JUST LITERACY:

Promoting Justice through Language and Learning

New York State English Council

John Harmon
Editor

Copyright 2002
New York State English Council
All Rights Reserved

Printed by

RICMAR
"the design and print shop"
101 Edson Street
Amsterdam, NY 12010

Cover photo
"A Just and Lasting Peace"
by
John Harmon

NCTE Information Exchange Agreement Member

New York State English Council Monographs

Just Literacy:

Promoting Justice through Language and Learning

edited by

John Harmon

New York State English Council
2002

TABLE OF CONTENTS

Introduction..i
    John Harmon

1. **Literacy and Social Responsibility: Democratic Principles in a Differentiated Classroom** 1
   Regina Dunlavey Derrico

   John Dewey 18

2. **Facing Teacher Fears About Lesbian and Gay Texts in The Classroom** 19
   Rob Linné

   William Shakespeare 39

3. **The Constructivist Classroom: An Antidote to Indifference**........................40
   Laurie Iodice

   Linda Darling-Hammond....................................57

4. **Re-Viewing Multicultural Sites: An Inquiry of Transcultural Betweenness**........................58
   Melissa Hasbrook

   Alexander Solzhenitsyn....................................88

5. Promoting Social Justice in the Young Adult
   Literature Class: Preparing Pre-Service
   Teachers to Choose Multicultural Texts............89
   Alice Trupe

   Gary Paulsen..106

6. Reflections on Language, Gender, Class,
   and Power Relations with Suggestions
   for Instructional Applications....................107
   Ines Senna Shaw

   Paolo Freire..139

7. Writers from the War Zone: Poets and the
   Literature of the Northern Ireland Troubles......140
   Maureen Murphy

   Meet the Authors..155

Introduction

John Harmon

The origins of **Justice** are many. This concept, which is a cornerstone in the development of all civilizations, finds one of its origins in the writings of Hesiod, approximately 2800 years ago. In his poem, *Works and Days*, Hesiod attributes to Zeus a particular distinction between animals and people. According to the poet, Zeus characterizes animals as "wild . . . for they have no **Justice**, but to human beings he has given **Justice**, which is far the best."

Although we try to infuse Justice into every phase of our lives, **Literacy** and **Literature** hold a special place for us, as well. Not only is the concept of Justice explored in a multitude of literary texts, teachers often rely on their study of language and literature to foster *democracy, equality*, and *plurality* in their classes, as well as in society.

As the twenty-first century dawned with unexpected anguish and terror, the concept of Justice leaped to the forefront of discussion and debates worldwide. Perhaps this topic was treated no more sensitively than in our nation's schools. In fact, thousands of teachers became the immediate providers of news, history, and compassion to millions of students who struggled to comprehend the unjust deaths of thousands of innocent people. Although teachers from every discipline faced the challenge of easing student tensions and reassuring fearful children, perhaps those whose work centers on language, literacy, and literature were especially well prepared. It is through the medium of language, the power of literacy, and the illumination of literature that we come to understand our complex, perplexing world.

For this book, teachers explored the many dimensions of Justice which permeate their English classes, their reading courses, their literature circles, and their teaching practices. They explored such broad questions as:

- What teaching practices promote both Justice and Literacy?
- How do we use Literature to promote Justice, Democracy, and Equality?
- How do we insure that the Literature which we study with our students is inclusive and pluralistic, representing the texture and diversity of our nation?

Perhaps the most uplifting aspect of their responses is that these writers did not dwell on the notion of Justice as the sword of retribution, punishing past wrongs. Rather, they envisioned the concept of Justice as a polestar, an "ever fixéd mark," guiding our teaching though the seas of tolerance, plurality, multiculturalism, and democracy.

Regina Derrico, for example, calls upon her experiences teaching in a "differentiated classroom" which brings together students of markedly different levels of achievement. Through a series of inspirational classroom anecdotes, Derrico demonstrates her commitment to providing an enriching, high quality education to *all* of her students. Guided by the writings of John Dewey, Derrico helps her students "view perplexity from a different perspective, and to see themselves as viable agents for solving problems." Derrico's success is measured not only in outstanding test scores or exemplary results on standardized assessments. More importantly, her students demonstrate their achievement through the genuine excitement they display in their own successes in reading and writing, as well as in the commitments they make to solving problems—often as a group—through their increasing proficiency in literacy.

Rob Linné reports on his ethnographic research which attempts not only illuminate, but to work against, a particular form of injustice. His study explores the fears and anxiety that many teachers report when they encounter—or consider—lesbian and gay texts in their classrooms. Again, Linné relies on the enormous power of language and literacy to influence, in sometimes very subtle ways, our thinking about sexuality. He also uses literature, especially those texts (including film and television) which are targeted to young adults, as a backdrop for his discussion of "typical, if messy, adolescent behavior." His research has led him to identify four rhetorical trends which provide the "most common features of resistance" to the idea of including gay and lesbian texts into our classrooms. He concludes his discussion with some practical suggestions for teachers who wish to explore further the possibilities of gay voices in the literature of our classrooms.

Laurie Iodice, another practicing teacher, relies on the writings of Dewey and Vygotsky, as well as a clearly inspirational staff development program in her own school, to develop a constructivist approach to her English classes. Iodice believes that "Constructivism promotes justice because it encourages a dialogic model." For example, this model "reaffirms the dangerous nature of tracking," "sees writing as a reflection and refraction of social conflicts," and "encourages successful group work." Iodice explores this model through the lens of an interdisciplinary course which combines elements of English and Global History.

Melissa Hasbrook's writing focuses on a particular dimension of Justice—pluralism. Through the medium of transculturalism, Hasbrook challenges teachers to pursue "social equality" and "democratic education." Relying on a wide range of educational philosophers for support, Hasbrook encourages us to see "the Nation(al) through a democratic frame, in part, embodied" by "Dewey's advocacy of individual opportunity to escape class boundaries." She also asks us to transform "blind nationalism" into "visible transculturalism," which acknowledges the complex cultural experiences reflected in the literature we study.

Alice Trupe provides us with numerous ways to promote social Justice through the careful selection of the texts we study with our students. Trupe focuses on the special needs of adolescents as she thoughtfully chooses multicultural works which appeal to young adults. Not only does she provide an engaging discussion of the challenge, Trupe also provides numerous titles, each with helpful annotations, as a resource for teachers as they fill their multicultural bookshelves.

Ines Shaw finds Justice in her reflections on "Language, Gender, Class, and Power Relations." Shaw warns us that the "sheer amount of daily exposure to gender, class, racial, dis/abilty, and sexual orientation biases" in our "discursive practices" has powerful, long-lasting effects on our worldview. Shaw provides plenty of interesting and powerful examples and anecdotes to support this view, including vivid memories of her own upbringing in Brazil. She concludes her writing by providing suggestions for classroom teachers who want to make connections between political power and literary study.

Maureen Murphy focuses on one particular culture—the Irish—for her contribution to the theme of Justice. The civil rights movement in Northern Ireland, of course, has a long and storied—or poetic—history. Murphy traces this struggle for civil rights through the poetry of Irish writers past and present. Murphy's thesis includes the powerful symbolism that language itself exerts on the development of a culture. "History as language/language as history has special implications for Ireland," Murphy contends. When one nation attempts to legislate the language of another, deep tensions and often violent conflicts are bound to erupt. For Murphy, the very language the writers chose to express their thoughts—English or Irish—was as much an important consideration as was the diction of the poem itself.

Each of these writers, therefore, demonstrates a commitment to social Justice in a deep and personal way. Yet, in the spirit of true democracy, each goes beyond his or her own personal interests to challenge all teachers to provide Justice for each and every student. Each of these contributors is, in the words of Todd DeStigter, a *citizen teacher*, "someone who understands his or her localized teaching practices as part of a broader project to promote democracy." And for many of us, we can think of no better way to promote democracy than through **Just Literacy**.

Literacy and Social Responsibility: Democratic Principles in a Differentiated Classroom

Regina Dunlavey Derrico

Rick, his head resting on the edge of his desk, was engaged in a serious study of his shoelace. Andy, maneuvering his fingerboard across the surface of his desk had morphed into pro skateboarder, Tony Hawk. Adriana of the beautiful blue eyes was murmuring something enticing to Jack who had long since abandoned all thoughts of Maycomb County and Mayella Ewell. And Kathi and I, well, in between feeble attempts to keep the discussion moving, were watching the clock, counting down the seconds until the end of fourth period.

Kathi Lederman, a special education teacher, and I were co-teaching a differentiated ninth grade English class. We were in trouble, and we knew it. Our students, particularly our special education students, had been struggling with the text of *To Kill A Mockingbird* for weeks. Until this point, their ability to connect their personal experiences to the events and characters in the book, as well as scaffolding activities which focused on reading strategies targeted at helping them to negotiate difficult aspects of the text, offered them the motivation and instructional support that they needed to persist with the text (Dewey, Vygotsky, Applebee). By the time they had reached chapter twenty-three, however, they were running out of steam. The community of learners which we had struggled to build was about to fall apart. For the first time since September, some students were unable to wholeheartedly participate in our conversations and class activities. So, they did what outsiders often do. They became silent, or adopted the views of other students, or initiated their own unrelated conversations. Lacking an appreciation for perplexity, disquietude and ambiguity — the bases of inquiry — they were shutting down (Dewey *How We Think*).

To help them view perplexity from a different perspective and to see themselves as viable agents for solving problems (Dewey *How We Think, Democracy and Education*), we developed a complex, task-oriented cooperative group activity. Choosing five chapters, (23-27), of *To Kill A Mockingbird*, we designed a jigsaw activity initially to move the students quickly through the text, yet also to give them a thorough understanding of the events and important ideas in that section of the novel. We assigned a heterogeneous group of five students to each chapter. Each group's goal was to read the assigned chapter, note the important developments in the plot and characters, make intratextual connections to other scenes, characters, themes in the text, and identify and learn any vocabulary words whose meaning could not be determined in context. After completing these tasks, each individual group member had to return to a base group of five other students, each of whom had been assigned to read a different chapter, and then teach that chapter to the other members of the group. To assess their understanding of the material, all the students in the class would take the same quiz covering details and events from all five chapters.

The stakes were high. No one wanted to be responsible for a less than perfect quiz score for any member of his group. When the students joined their reading groups, they set about developing a plan of action to meet their group goal. Everyone had to be listened to;

everyone's suggestions had to be considered. Would they spend the two days they had to complete the assignment by reading the text aloud to the group? If so, who would read aloud? Only the most proficient readers? Or should everyone take a turn? Should they read part of the chapter in class and the remainder for homework? Before they began to highlight their text, should they review the reading strategies that they had been working with throughout the unit? Which of the reading strategies did they think would be most appropriate? And how were they going to record their information to prepare for their discussion of the chapter? Should they take notes? Write a response log? Create a graphic organizer? Finally, were they going to develop a common presentation to take to their individual base groups or should each member be responsible for organizing his own presentation? Which if any passages from the chapter should be read aloud to their base groups to substantiate their points about the chapter?

Formerly bubble-headed Adriana became the taskmaster of her group. "All right, take out your planners and write this down: finish chapter 25 for homework." Jack, too, initiated some action. "OK, I'll begin reading the chapter aloud so we can get a sense of who's who and what's going on." As Jack began to read, Andy, unsure of what had happened in the previous chapters said, "Wait. Wait. Who's this Maudie chick again?"

Actively engaged in collaborative groups to complete a common goal, our students were being socialized for adult roles. Democratic principles such as fairness, equality, and responsibility were clearly at play (Dewey *Democracy and Education*).

Finally with the group activities completed and the quizzes taken, Betsy raised her hand and commented, "I wonder what would have happened to Burris and the other Ewell kids if they had done a group activity on the first day of school. Maybe they would have come back the next day."

"Yeah," added Melinda, "Maybe things wouldn't have seemed so hopeless that day when Mayella was on the witness stand."

"And maybe, if she believed she was a part of the community, she would have told the truth," sighed Tony.

This thoughtful speculation propelled us into a very serious discussion focusing on the broader concept of social responsibility that permeates the novel. We discussed the problems that often result when people for whatever reason—gender, race, religion, social status, or even academic ability—are marginalized and pushed to the fringes of society. We discussed the importance of developing communities which value a diversity of perspectives and celebrate differences. We enriched our understanding of our own differentiated English class by examining it through the lens of the text we were reading.

Since the mid-1980s, inspired by the work of John Goodlad and Jeannie Oakes, we have been grouping our students heterogeneously in a very broad sense of the word. Students in our English 9 program are grouped heterogeneously by ability level. Students in our 10-12 English program are also grouped heterogeneously—mixing students across three grade levels (tenth, eleventh and twelfth), and mixing students of various ability levels (low achieving through high achieving). Our students, with the help of their teachers and parents, identify themselves by ability level according to five phases. We seek this identification to ensure a proper mix of students in each class. A class with too many high-achieving students and too few low-achieving students would not provide the heterogeneity we seek, nor allow us to implement the instructional strategies and practices which promote the cooperative community of learners which we know is most effective to learning for all our students.

Proponents of ability grouping often question our move to heterogeneous grouping, expressing their concerns that we have "dumbed down" our curriculum and, assuming that we "teach to the middle," fail to challenge our high achieving, "gifted" students. They fear, too, that our low achieving, "at-risk" students are not being given attainable goals and the extra instructional support that they need. Our response is that ability grouping is unfair to low achievers. Far too often, low teacher expectations, emphasis on drill-and-practice instructional strategies, and poor peer models are problems characteristic of low ability groups. But when all students are exposed to interesting and challenging educational experiences which promote active engagement, the low-achieving student will demand assistance and explanation, usually from her classmates. In turn, the high-achieving student will solidify her own learning by explaining materials and sharing problem-solving methodologies with her classmates (Cohen *Designing Group Work*).

Simply grouping students heterogeneously, however, will not enhance learning. Understanding how learning best occurs and developing a pedagogy based on that understanding is essential to maintaining effective heterogeneous grouping. Recognizing that learning is a social activity, that students are drawn naturally into learning from one another regardless of ability level, we implement a wide range of instructional strategies and practices which take advantage of the various strengths that our students bring to their classes. For example, rather than clustering our students into ability groups within the classroom, we emphasize cooperative learning, enabling our students to work in small heterogeneous learning groups to complete a definite group goal. Students bring multiple perspectives and a wide range of skills to these groups. As they engage in task-oriented interaction to help one another meet their academic goal, identify problems and develop plans of action to further explore and solve those problems, their differences become assets, not liabilities.

Other important nonacademic benefits result from such grouping as well. Placed in a situation in which they must confront differences in past experiences and caches of prior knowledge, a range of skills and dispositions toward learning, and varying modalities of learning, students develop a thoughtful respect for the many dimensions of diversity which in turn improves the self-esteem of all students. Not relying on an outside authority figure to tell them what to do and how to do it, they develop a habit of inquiry and a sense of commitment and responsibility, control and ownership, important to their development as active citizens in a multi-cultural society (Dewey *How We Think*). As a department we are very proud of the inclusive nature of our program and our refusal to track our students. In the spirit of Frank Smith, we have extended membership to the literacy club to all of our students. Well, at least most of them.

Until this past year, only some of our special education students, those requiring the least amount of instructional support in language arts, were mainstreamed into our classes. The others, those labeled as self-contained, were not a part of our program. Instead, they were grouped into classes of no more than fifteen students which were taught by teachers holding a degree in special education, not English. Every year we would tell the special education teachers what books we would be teaching and they would choose those which seemed most appropriate to the reading levels of their students, and modify or jettison those which seemed too difficult. For example, when our students studied Shakespeare which they do every spring, the special education students would study the same play. Their version of the text, however, retold the plot in language which denied them the richness and beauty of Shakespeare's diction. The complexity, wit, and humor of his word play were somehow deemed too difficult for these low-achieving students. While our students spent weeks transforming their classrooms into working theatres, working as a community to meet its goal of producing a segment of the play, they could only stand by and ask, "Why can't we do that?" While our students wrote poetry and prose pieces in response to art work secured from the Albright Knox Art Gallery (displayed each month in a central area in our school); while our students read and wrote poetry, and extended their understanding of the printed word by building on their individual interests in music, art, dance and created music compositions, paintings and sculptures, and choreographed dance performances, these special education students wrote and rewrote topic sentences, hammered out introductory paragraphs, and were involved in test-prep activities intended to help them pass the state mandated, high-stakes 11th grade English Regents exam. Although these experiences were well-intended, they were "mis-educative" in that instead of generating new experiences, they had the effect of "arresting and distorting the growth of further experience" (Dewey *Experience and Education* 28).

Of course, this was not the fault of the special education teachers. They could only work with what they had. An authentic community is a diverse community. Neither our special education teacher colleagues nor their students had truly been invited to join the literacy club.

Our district's move to differentiated instruction made it possible for everyone, students and teachers alike, to not only accept the invitation, but to participate fully in the literacy experiences of our program. For the first time, as a teacher, I had the opportunity to work daily alongside a specialist who could offer effective strategies for working with special needs students. And for the first time that specialist could rely on the expertise of a content area teacher. Together, we could work side-by-side, learning from one another, honing our instructional skills and refining our classroom practices to better meet the needs of all our students.

In reality, however, things did not work out exactly as we envisioned them. Our enrollment numbers denied us the balance that would add to our success. When I had agreed to work with a special education teacher and co-teach a differentiated ninth grade classes, I had been assured that no more than seven special education students would be in the mix. I had also been assured that class size would be held to a maximum of twenty-two. Instead, the class consisted of twenty-nine students, thirteen of whom were receiving special education services. Both Kathi and I knew that building a sense of community, overcoming the biases that tracking and labeling students generates, had to be our first priority (Cohen *Designing Group Work*). Many of our students were very uneasy that first month of school. The honors level students were reluctant to be placed in groups with kids whose prowess they respected outside the academic classroom—on the soccer field or in photography club—but with whom they had never discussed a book or shared a piece of writing. And the special education students were wary, too. They knew, only too well, how they were perceived. They were believed to be kids who didn't take their schoolwork seriously. They certainly never read and they definitely couldn't write. But, Kathi and I were undaunted; exploring unfamiliar territory, yet each possessing a wealth of survival skills we forged ahead, sometimes cautiously, while at other times recklessly.

From the beginning, Kathi and I had decided that we would minimize the overt indicators of differentiation as much as possible. Although we had each received separate class lists—mine identifying all the regular education students, hers all the special education students—we decided not to keep separate attendance records. She alphabetized both lists into one common list, making a copy for me to keep in my plan book. Kathi took attendance every day as I organized the class for the day's activities, reminding students to place their planners and notebooks on their desks, directing them into their writing groups, sometimes asking them to move into a large group for a literature discussion. In order to limit the possibility of students' being positioned by the status roles—academic, peer, societal—which they may have carried with them from their elementary/middle school experiences, we relied on flexible grouping, increasing the interaction among different students, matching students' abilities to specific instructional activities.

We did not change our curriculum from that of the rest of the ninth grade program. All of our students were required to study the same texts and engage in similar writing activities. They read and wrote for a variety of purposes and explored a variety of forms, just as every other student in the ninth grade program did. How our students approached their work, the instructional strategies and classroom practices that we implemented, the time devoted to particular areas of study may have been different, yet all of our students had the same opportunities as every other student.

As we planned and developed our lessons, I relied on a few beliefs that had guided my work with heterogeneous classes for over fifteen years. Obviously influenced by Dewey, I believe that an effective curriculum needs to constantly draw on students' interests and experiences in order to trigger inquiry into broader themes, issues and concepts. Our students moved through our first text, Suzanne Fisher Staples' *Shabanu*. It is not a particular difficult text to read. Relating it to prior knowledge and experience, in this case family dynamics, gave all our students a way into the novel. By exploring a much broader idea—the tensions that exist when the needs and desires of the individual conflict with those of the group— our students were able to extend and expand their thinking, bringing a variety of perspectives to their discussion of the text.

We began our study of *Shabanu* by viewing a few clips from the film *Clueless* and asking our students to focus on the film's portrayal of American teenagers. In their learning log, a place where they reflect on their literacy experiences, we asked them to write a response exploring how a person from another culture might perceive American teenagers and cultural values based on this film. The following day we placed our students in cooperative learning groups. Our obvious goal was to provide our students with the opportunity to share their responses to the film. Everyone had viewed the clips (all but one student had seen the film in its entirety one or more times). Of course, as teenagers themselves, everyone had interest and experience and, therefore, something to say. Our underlying goal was a social one. In her book, *Designing Group Work, Strategies for the Heterogeneous Classroom*, Elizabeth Cohen documents the social benefits of group work, noting that, "When people work together on cooperative tasks, they are more likely to form friendly ties, to trust each other, and to influence each other than when the task stimulates competition among members" (14).

This group activity was followed by another in which the students generated a list of assumptions about American teenagers implied by the film. The students then developed a list of sources which an individual might consult as a way of gaining more information in order to test his inferences about American teenagers. From this point, we moved to a whole class discussion of an essential concept—our effective functioning as a community of learners. We knew that to function effectively as a class, and for our students to function as effective adults in a democratic society, that it would be important for all of our students to develop necessary skills—listening to others and working with the ideas of others—as they learned to carry on productive, organized discussions to explore concepts and issues and to solve problems. This practice of suspending judgment, of being willing to look at differences with an open-mind, and exploring the reasons for those differences became one of the broad concepts which focused our literature study for the entire year.

The news stories which both preceded and followed the events of September 11th further piqued our students' curiosity, interest, and compassion. The treatment of women under the Taliban, the intricacies of Islamic culture, the geography of the Pakistan/Afghanistan border all related directly to our discussions of the text. Our discussions were lively and often, argumentative. Whether or not our students would label it as a great read, they left the text with more questions than answers and a bit more curious about the world beyond their world.

The three texts which followed, however, were far more challenging. Although the literature on differentiated instruction suggests that approaches to texts may often be modified—students may read an abridged or altered form of a text, listen to the text on tape, view the film if one exists (Tomlinson *The Differentiated Classroom*)—Kathi and I did not want to do that. We provided our students with the extra support and resources they needed. Kathi met with those students whose Individual Education Plans required them to receive additional instructional support every day. During that time she often read difficult sections of the text to them and occasionally showed them segments of the film to help them visualize characters and events. We wanted to help our students—*all of them*, not just those designated as special education students—to internalize strategies that would increase their ability to read difficult texts. We built support or scaffolding activities into our tasks so that our students could internalize new knowledge, skills, and strategies for use with other learning situations (Vygotsky *Mind in Society*).

Recognizing that fluency is essential to developing increased reading ability, we encouraged our students to read texts that related to the themes in the required texts. So, in addition as outside reading books, while engaged in their study of *To Kill A Mockingbird*, our students were encouraged to read Gary Paulsen's *Night John* and Christopher Paul Curtis's *The Watsons Go To Birmingham*, as well as Mildred Taylor's *Roll of Thunder, Hear My Cry*, Richard Wright's *Black Boy*, and Cynthia Voight's *The Runner*, and James McBride's *The Color of Water*. Since our students engage in sustained silent reading for forty-two minutes every Friday, many chose to read these books during that time. Informal literature circles were forming as students made choices, swapped books, and made connections to ideas discussed in class.

Some students, however, resisted the book titles we suggested. Instead they whined, "Why can't we ever read any good books?" Kathi and I were disappointed. We had been trying so hard to gather materials which we felt would address our students' interests and levels of ability. We had no choice but to ask, "Well, what are some good books you think we should be reading?" In less than ten minutes the class had generated a list of titles, among them Chris Lynch's *Iceman*, Laurie Halse Anderson's *Speak*,

Patricia McCormick's *Cut* and Louis Sachar's *Holes*. When Kathi discovered some left over money in her book budget, we purchased multiple copies of several of these titles. The students eagerly moved through these books.

It is important to note that for every one of our successes there were easily ten failures. And some of our special education students, especially Marty and Carl, found assimilating into our heterogeneous class and working comfortably in small groups very difficult. Neither boy appeared to have any characteristic to give him status in a group. Neither played sports, had demonstrated a talent in art or music, or was a member of the in-crowd. Physically, they were at the extreme ends of the group. Carl was big and burly. With his mass of curly blond hair and his leather battle jacket, he could easily have passed for a freshman in college. His sidekick, Marty, was just the opposite. A short, roly-poly kid with a moonbeam smile, he looked like he hadn't yet completed sixth grade. Socially, they never fit in. At first they resisted the group activities, refused to follow through on the roles assigned them, and seldom did any homework which was directly related to group activities. Because the activities we designed required every individual to participate, Carl and Marty eventually became sharers and partners in the group's activities. The successes of the group became their successes and its failures their failures (Dewey *Democracy and Education*). Although it took them longer than the other students to see themselves, as valuable contributors to their groups, eventually they did. In turn, each developed a positive disposition toward his own learning, an awareness of his own academic strengths and a willingness to struggle with his academic weaknesses.

The school year ended with our study of *Romeo and Juliet*. Keeping the needs of our gifted students in mind, and wanting to build on the success of our cooperative group activities, Kathi and I decided to introduce the whole class to a very challenging writing activity. Presenting the class with a passage from the play, we told the students that we were going to look at Shakespeare's diction, his word choice, try to identify a controlling image pattern, and then discuss how the language increased our understanding of character and theme. Such a passage analysis is a sophisticated task even for high-achieving students. Our students were nervous, but excited to begin. Their interest in the play was high. They knew exactly how Romeo and Juliet felt as they navigated their way through adolescent love, unruly friends and controlling adults. Because of their literacy experiences throughout the year, they were comfortable discussing and writing about literature. And they trusted Kathi and me, as well as their peers, to give them the instructional support needed to complete their task. Once again, Kathi and I designed a complex cooperative group activity to provide the scaffolding our students would need to complete the task. Several days later, after the task had been completed and the writing shared, we threw out the challenge. We asked out students to focus on a different passage and repeat the entire activity, this time on their own. We designated two class days as time to work individually on the task, but the students would have to spend time at home in order to compete the assignment on time. During that two-day period, Kathi and I offered students any additional instructional support needed.

The day the assignment was due, I pulled into the school parking lot. A bit confused, I noticed that only a handful of students was gathered outside of school and that there was not a school bus in sight. Because the school had experienced a major power outage, classes had been cancelled for the day. As I entered the building, I saw Marty. I asked him if he wanted to use my cell phone to call home for a ride. "Sure, but before I do, can I show you my passage analysis? It's really good. I really like the way I ended it. I said that to make the play work, we have to believe in love at first sight. I'm pretty proud of that," he beamed. And how proud I was of him. Through his active experiences working with others, Marty developed habits and dispositions which not only shaped his attitude toward learning, but also led to an ability to readjust his activity to meet new conditions and confront perplexing situations (Dewey *Democracy and Education*). At long last, Marty had claimed his place in our community of learners.

Democracy is predicated on participation. *Just literacy* demands creating educational environments which allow *all* our students to participate meaningfully as valued members of a community of learners. Although it is a complex and often arduous task, it is our moral responsibility to ensure that all students will have access to the skills and knowledge necessary for them to assume their roles as fully contributing and participating citizens in our democratic society.

Works Cited

Applebee, Arthur. "Engaging Students in the Disciplines of English: What Are Effective Schools Doing?" *English Journal.* 91 (6), 30-36.

Cohen, Elizabeth. *Designing Group Work: Strategies for Heterogeneous Classrooms.* New York: Teachers College Press, 1987.

Dewy, John. *Democracy and Education: An Introduction to the Philosophy of Education.* 1916. New York: Macmillan, 1985.

----------. *Experience and Education.* 1938. New York: Collier, 1969.

----------. *How We Think.* 1910. New York: Dover Publications, 1997.

Tomlinson, Ann. *The Differentiated Classroom.* Alexandria, VA: ASCD, 1999.

Vygotsky, Lev. *Mind in Society: The Development of Higher Psychological Processes.* Cambridge: Harvard University Press, 1980.

It is the aim of progressive education to take part in correcting unfair privilege and unfair deprivation, not to perpetuate them.

John Dewey

Democracy and Education

Facing Teacher Fears About Lesbian and Gay Texts in the Classroom

Rob Linné

High schools may be the most homophobic institutions in American society. ~Gerald Unks

In recent years the complete disregard for lesbians and gays in education has been challenged. Students have begun agitating for more safe and inclusive schools (Pemberton-Butler) and some teachers have pioneered gay-friendly curriculums and classroom environments (Greenbaum). In our field—English Education—teachers now have more choices of quality books and films that speak to gay issues or experiences as well as surveys of the literature to help guide them through their choices (Linné). And yet, despite the increased availability of texts and resources, relatively few teachers have introduced gay and lesbian voices into their curriculums. Even among the teachers I work with in New York City, most remain reticent to even peek inside the classroom closet. The initial reactions of my "seen it all" urban teachers to the idea of adolescent literature with gay themes surprised me somewhat as I expected college educated professionals living and working in the city that conceived the modern Gay Rights movement to be more at ease with the subject. When my efforts were countered with stronger resistance than I expected, I realized that we in the field of English Education still need to focus much more on preparing teachers for gay issues in school before the reading of novels even begins. The censorship that silences any talk of sexuality and youth remains powerful even in this age of

Will & Grace and Rosie O'Donnell. Although the vast majority of teachers want to do the right thing for all of our students, change remains slow because the educational system does not respond quickly to change and offers few models for new ways of thinking and speaking about sexual minorities.

This research report represents my attempts to reach a deeper understanding of the obstacles teachers face when they begin contemplating gay-friendly curriculums and classrooms. I begin with language. Because educational discourse structures so many firewalls protecting the hetero-normative, it becomes necessary to unpack all of the assumptions inherent in the language used to discuss (or not discuss) sexuality in schools. By getting specific about the anti-gay rhetoric typical of educationese, I believe more effective pedagogical counter-moves can be implemented. In this analysis I attempt to make overt the implicit anti-gay rhetoric of schools and schooling, as well as explore specific pedagogical methods that bring the prejudices of our system out into the open.

My inquiry has led to a sociolinguistic discourse analysis of teachers discussing the possibilities or impossibilities of including lesbian and gay voices or texts in the English Language Arts curriculum. My methods of research follow in the traditions of qualitative studies in education and sociolinguistic analysis (Merriam). I collected data including class discussions and individual journals as well as essays for discourse analysis from participants in a secondary literacy course comprised of New York City teachers working on their graduate degrees.

Theoretical Background

Sociolinguist James Gee's work clearly resonates with any research looking into the ways educational institutions use language as an anti-democratic force. Gee contends that ideology is always wrapped up in our discourses, the subtle ways individuals are taught what or whom to value, not necessarily by what is openly said, but by the way it is said, or by what is left unsaid. Gee's work suggests that we remain complicit, especially as educators, in maintaining inequities and prejudices by allowing assumptions about marginalized people to go unexamined among our colleagues and students. Usually false stereotypes or prejudices go unchallenged by leaving certain groups or individuals out of "our" collective stories, as when one culture is left out of the school canon or curriculum. Sociolinguistic work takes on a process of reading between the lines to make explicit the power dynamics implicit in institutionalized language.

I rarely encounter teachers who react with blatant homophobia to my inquiries in this area. A few have walked out of the class during the viewing of a scene from a PG rated teen coming-out film, and others have vented anger over even being asked to consider gay texts. However, most teachers want to be fair to all of their students and attempt to approach the subject with an open mind. Most of the teachers I have worked with claim to hold no prejudice against gays, and want to consider ways they can improve the chances or aspirations of our gay youth.

Yet moving empathy to action remains difficult because teachers as a group simply do not yet have a shared language that gives them confidence to make new voices heard. For the most part, the only scripts offered those in the field of education are either timid liberal notions of "tolerance" or the more forceful reactionary rhetorics of a conservative backlash. Educational discourse has quickly co-opted much of this dialog that has taken place out in the larger culture as a means to avoid difficult change. The teacher talk I analyzed often followed very similar patterns of anti-gay rhetoric despite my teachers' desires not to be homophobic. When the false assumptions of these rhetorics are laid bare most educators are disappointed with the lack of guidance they have been given by the educational system and demonstrate a willingness to seek change.

In the next section I outline the most common features of resistance I have found in the discourse of education. The four rhetorical trends I document are **clinical containment, public/private dichotomy, transcendence,** and **bureaucratic power**.

Clinical Containment

The first pattern that emerged in our class discussions was a very clinical "diagnosis" of (homo)sexual youth, rather than a social construction of the whole person in cultural contexts. Clinical containment works to keep gay issues out of the curriculum by circumscribing homosexuality as the domain of mental health professionals. Such a construction applies only to gay youth, never to straight youth. For example, in my adolescent literacy course I ask students to reflect on the books that were important to them as teens. During the semester that began this study, as with most, much of the conversation was dominated by narratives about books centered on sexual awakenings. For example, many females remembered vividly how crucial books addressing adolescent coming-of-age issues such as Judy Blume's *Forever* were to their development. Male students, although not as often as the females, also reported searching in books or magazines for answers to questions about their changing bodies and desires. When I asked the class if they knew of any books young gays might use for similar explorations, no suggestions were offered.

    To explore this lack further, the next week I showed parts of *Beautiful Thing*, a gay coming-of-age film. This British import is very tame compared to Hollywood teen films. Gratuitous sex and "wild teen behavior" are noticeably lacking, and the characters are quite thoughtfully developed. However, the class discussion first focused on the sex, what little of it was alluded to in the film. Students noted "surprise [at] watching a film with sex as a theme" and uncertainty as to "whether this film is too adult for secondary literacy." Such reactions were paradoxical in light of the fact that we had read texts or viewed films where (straight) sexual exploration was foregrounded more vividly. Sexual awakening as a topic is unavoidable in young adult literature as current adolescent novels offer more graphic depictions of sexuality than a typical night of HBO. The teachers in this course, however, never questioned the appropriateness of the sexuality in the more explicit straight coming-of-age stories.

    Similarly, the discussion participants strained to diagnose potential causes for the characters' sexual explorations. Almost half the class focused on the dysfunctional elements of the protagonists' families or social environments and several speculated that these problems caused the boys' homosexuality, their "experimentations," or even their assumed sexual "confusion." For example, one student began her response with, "the two [boys] were trying to escape their bad family lives by finding comfort in each other." Others suggested the boys were perhaps "trying out different sexualities" as a means of avoiding the reality of their lives. Again, such readings conflicted with teacher analyses of straight texts. The canon of adolescent literature is full of dysfunctional families, substance abuse, and violence, yet when reading adolescent "problem novels" populated with straight protagonists, my class did not tend towards as much psychoanalysis in order to explain what is "wrong" with the characters. Usually, character actions or conflicts are accepted more readily as "teen behavior," motivated by typical, if messy, adolescent development.

Kirk Fuoss contends that a clinical construct contains sexuality as simply a discreet behavior rather than an important aspect of each individual's identity or our culture's diversity (166). All of the life experiences a young gay person goes through in a homophobic society, as well as all the affirmative aspects gay culture has developed in response, are ignored by this limited and limiting view. One effect is that we attempt to keep our gay youth invisible and in the closet. As long as (homo)sexuality remains just a physical act or an isolatable psychological problem or "confusion," it can remain on the periphery of our consciousness as something controllable or hopefully even reversible. We as educators then do not have to get involved.

A willingness to keep the issues of gay youth contained inside the medical and outside the educational, manifested in many teachers' suggestions for addressing lesbian and gay issues. Many in my class compared teen homosexuality to other adolescent "problems" such as drug abuse, alcohol abuse, AIDS, teen sex, or teen pregnancy. A clinical response such as this gives gay students the message that they are inherently dysfunctional—not the most affirming self-image for young people to build upon. After categorizing sexual orientation with health and welfare issues, several teachers suggested that the appropriate places to address gay issues include only the school counselor's or psychologist's office, a life skills course, or sex education and AIDS prevention classes. The English classroom, from this perspective, is excluded as a site for exploration of gay social, cultural, or psychological themes and issues.

One teacher's comment summed up teacher concerns in this regard: "I am not a sex educator. I would have no idea where to begin talking about sex with my students let alone homosexuality." Another teacher countered with, "But as was mentioned earlier, you don't have to talk about sex. We are talking about respect and understanding people that may be different."

Public/Private Dichotomy

The public/private dichotomy limits any talk of lesbians of gays to the home or the therapist's couch. If you have spent any time at all in a middle school or high school lately you have heard homophobic put-downs like "fag", "dyke," or "queer" shouted through the halls or spit out on the athletic fields. Anti-gay slurs have become so common that many students even report teachers who are unconcerned about displaying their own homophobia through put-downs or jokes (GLSEN). Sometimes the words are meant to inflict serious wounds, especially among adolescent boys. For a boy to be labeled a "fag" in school can lead to serious ostracism, even physical abuse. Other times the epitaphs aren't meant quite so maliciously, as when one girl tells another not to buy a certain pair of shoes because they are "way too gay." Yet the words retain their power as social boundary markers nevertheless. No matter the intention, anti-gay language now takes up a central space in adolescent discourse both in school and out.

  Media culture aimed at teen audiences has become obsessed with gay sexuality as a resonating trope. Teen film comedies use homophobic humor as a stock reference point for easy laughs; day time talk shows frequently host "shocking" episodes focusing on young sexual minorities; and television wrestling stars frequently beat up on flamboyant, stereotypically "gay" villains to the cheers of the mostly teen audiences.

  The current ubiquity of discursive gay bashing using language that was more taboo for earlier generations of young people begs the question: Why is this language of hate becoming so loud in this day and age among our young people? The answer may be found in the dynamics of cultural change and confusion, as well as the backlash that inevitably follows the increased visibility which civil rights struggles always bring to oppressed people.

Young people today are players in a complex social drama with very little direction from adults. The scripts are changing dramatically regarding sexualities and the upheaval can be confusing for youth. One day young people are witness to progressive images such as a television show centered on gay lives (*Will & Grace*), while the next day elements of the backlash may take the movement two steps back (as when evangelist Pat Robertson recently suggested the September 11 attacks could be blamed on feminists and lesbians and gays in New York). Our students demonstrate more and more vividly just how confused they are with all the contradictions by acting out in ways that young people do when they have a need, an issue, a big question they want addressed. A psychoanalytic reading of the culture suggests youth are engaging in so much homophobic language, joking and innuendo as an indirect way of calling attention to their questions, and they will continue until adults join the conversation.

This group dissonance is met largely with silence from the adults charged with socializing our youth, including teachers, coaches, and counselors. Although some schools and individual teachers are beginning to intervene when they hear the name calling, relatively few have yet to move beyond the reactive to a deeper proactive dialog that would comprehensively address issues of gender and sexuality. The first explanation offered for such reticence is the fear of "opening up a whole new Pandora's Box" by "introducing this subject" to their students. Despite the current spotlight on lesbian and gay issues in adolescent discourse, media, and culture, the claim that young people are ignorant of the current cultural firmament continues to hold weight.

Teachers in the study expressed many fears regarding the discomfort that the introduction of this topic would cause to their students. Teachers were concerned that their students "would freak out" and "not be able to handle the subject with respect." Teachers also questioned their abilities to manage the discussion with groups of young people. "I would probably make matters worse once my students started laughing and making fun of the characters in the book." "My students are not mature enough." "This topic is too tricky to discuss with kids in a group. Maybe one-to-one, in private, would be better."

Private discussions between a student and a teacher or a student and a counselor struck many in my class as the safest or most appropriate arena. Some suggested that issues of sexual orientation were too personal for educators to take up with their students. These teachers (working from a clinical construct) defined sexual orientation as a private, moral issue that parents should decide when and how to discuss with their children. For teachers to engage students in dialog about lesbians and gays would amount to usurping parental authority and challenging the morals parents want their children to hold.

One teacher contended that our jobs as English teachers do not include the teaching of morality. Almost half the teachers seemed to agree by suggesting that lesbian or gay issues did not really fall under the domain of the English Language Arts classroom. Again, a double standard could be argued to exist because students in this class had embraced the ideals of personal response to texts as espoused by reader response theorists as well as the goals of personal development espoused by proponents of young adult literature. Similarly, the class had demonstrated strong support for the social and civil goals of literature study. Literature class was viewed by most as an acceptable space for exploring issues of marginalized groups such as women and ethnic or religious minorities. Progressive English classrooms were understood to be places where young readers could learn to better understand others by virtually living through the personal experiences of individual characters.

As our conversation unfolded, some teachers noted the contradictions inherent in any rhetorical move that attempts to censor personal explorations in the literature classroom. One noted: "Of course sexual preference is an issue many people are still uncomfortable with. Even some of the teachers in this room. However, it is a real life issue and we have talked all semester about motivating kids with real life issues that affect them. Literature gives us the opportunities." Another reinforced the importance of addressing lesbians and gays in the curriculum: "Judging by all the gay-bashing and prejudice among our students, we would clearly be negligent to avoid addressing such an important issue."

Transcendence

The complete inverse of the public/private dichotomy is the notion of transcendence. Transcendence suggests that our culture has now moved beyond prejudice of lesbian and gay youth and so there is no need for discussion in the school. The assumptions underlying this rhetoric suggest that our society has transcended any past problems with prejudice against gay people and so it follows that one's sexuality is a not an issue. From this perspective, a person's sexuality does not play an important enough role in a person's life story so to focus attention on sexual orientation would be akin to obsessing over any other detail of one's physical body such as eye color or height. The conflicting rhetorics of the public/private dichotomy and transcendence trap teachers in a double bind that limits the possibilities for discussion on two fronts. On the one hand, we in education are saying sexuality does not matter. To be gay is "no big deal," just one small detail among many that some people have to deal with. On the other hand, we are saying sexuality matters too much. Sexual orientation is such an explosive topic that we could never talk about it with young people without causing chaos in the classroom and disrupting the whole learning process.

One teacher summed up the transcendent paradigm: "I also think it shouldn't be this isolated issue of being gay. Just because you have a different sexual preference why are we going to make it an issue? Non-issues of respect and diversity would be a way of handling this without giving more attention to certain groups."

Much of this discourse could probably be traced to the rhetoric of "special rights" that has developed in response to increasing visibility of lesbians and gays. Conservative critics of gay rights have argued that sexual preference is an irrelevant issue that some people are attempting to exploit in order to gain extra privileges or advantages. From this perspective, even bringing up the topic of sexuality is counter-productive because gay people already have access to the same rights and privileges as straight people. By discussing gays and lesbians we are complicit in the process of creating a new minority.

A liberal perspective, although coming from a different paradigm, can end up at the same conclusion as a conservative perspective. Some teachers expressed a desire to demonstrate their solidarity with lesbians and gays by ignoring them. Teacher comments suggested that to acknowledge gay people would amount to exposing gay youth to discrimination that they wanted to shield them from. Some teachers said that they, "see all of [their] students as the same when they walk into [their] classrooms." One argued that she "did not want to make any of [her] students feel different." Teachers operating from this paradigm believe that "tolerance" and an erasure of difference is the most effective means of countering all forms of prejudice.

Although this rhetoric has grown out of a desire to combat all prejudices by teaching young people that "we are all the same," the discourse is flawed because it lacks credibility with young people. They can see the realities of societal prejudices played out in their schools and communities on a daily basis. Even though multicultural theorists have long critiqued the limits of curriculums seeking "tolerance" as ineffective at best, counter-productive at worst (hooks 39) the language of tolerance continues to be the dominant paradigm in our schools. The "hidden curriculum" of tolerance may teach young people that it is not acceptable to make fun of gay people in front of authorities, but neither is it really acceptable to be gay. For if gay people, especially gay youth, were truly accepted, teachers would do more than offer the right to be left alone. We would demonstrate that gay students as well as students with gay parents or siblings are honored or valued just as much as the next student by including their lives in all that we do (Sedgwick 32-34). Tolerance does not equal respect and most young people know from experience the vast gulf separating the two concepts.

Bureaucratic Power

The last rhetorical gate built into educational discourse is that of bureaucratic power. The rhetoric of bureaucratic power absolves us as educators from any complicity in reproducing homophobia by placing all blame on the institution.

Even after teachers have worked their way through the blind spots inherent in the other rhetorics, many have a difficult time seeing any way around the powerful argument that they could lose their jobs if they upset the bureaucracy. Teachers in this study did not feel empowered to make changes in their curriculums even if they felt the changes were important or necessary. Myriad fears and concerns about their positions in the bureaucracy were cited as to why whatever "should be done never would be in [the] schools. "

One teacher's worries seemed representative of the group's: "On the one hand we probably do have gay students in our classes and we do not address them. On the other hand, will "They" let us read things of this nature? I myself am reluctant to include discussions like this after a teacher here in the city was harassed and almost lost her job because she read *Nappy Hair*. It makes you wonder, is it really worth the loss of my job, which is everything to me, to include this in the curriculum?"

Many teachers were under the impression that the New York City school board has written explicit rules about not addressing or even speaking about lesbians and gays. "These issues are still untouchables for teachers in the classroom. We are not allowed to talk about gay concerns and the Board only allows guidance counselors to address this issue. Therefore, even if we wanted to have an all inclusive classroom our jobs do not allow it." Although no teachers knew where these rules were written and no one had been warned by their principles not to touch this subject, most teachers strongly believed that there must be regulations somewhere that would not allow open discussion in their classrooms.

The anti-gay rhetoric underlying educational discourse in American schools is so strong that the bureaucracy does not have to be at all explicit regarding lesbians and gays. Teachers self-censor themselves so the system does not have to.

Implications for Classroom Practice

As I have attempted pedagogical moves that would demonstrate alternatives to the homophobic practices of traditional schooling, a deeper understanding of the rhetorics outlined above has helped me focus my efforts. I offer the following teaching methods as examples of ways the silences surrounding sexuality can be addressed in the English Language Arts classroom. These techniques offer teachers a chance to learn a language of inclusion that moves beyond the traditional language of exclusion. I can only offer anecdotal support for these methods as I have not yet undertaken a follow-up study to see how teachers may translate these pedagogies into their secondary classrooms.

In my class I now begin with a character study of a protagonist in an adolescent coming-of-age novel. Using common techniques found in many reader-response based English classrooms, such as character maps and journal reflections, I ask students to map out all of the influences on the character's life and to attempt to trace the character's motivations back to possible sources. Inevitably, we find that it is impossible to disregard any single aspect of a character's identity—her race, class background, gender, family dynamics, or sexuality—if one wants to understand the whole character. Sexuality, especially proves to be the focus of development for any adolescent facing coming-out while coming-of-age. Characters in adolescent literature and film teach us that sexuality is not simply a physical act, but a central component of identity, especially for those young people who live outside of mainstream norms.

In a similar vein, I seek to problematize the notion that we have transcended issues of sexuality in our culture by focusing on many of the issues young lesbians or gays face on a daily basis. After listening to violently homophobic lyrics in hip-hop or rock popular with teens, we discuss possible reasons for the recent increases in gay bashing among young people. We also look at quantitative statistics that reveal the high rates of harassment or violence young gays are subjected to by peers or parents, and the increased rates of substance abuse, homelessness, dropping out, and even suicide correlated with societal rejection of young gays. Personal narratives written by young gay people are used to illustrate first hand the myriad prejudices and obstacles young people must still overcome as they negotiate society from an oppressed position. Such texts demonstrate that sexuality does matter to young people even if it would be much easier for us in education if the problem were already solved. Guest speakers such as gay youth from local high school gay/straight student alliances or community gay youth centers have offered powerful testimonies to my classes and strong motivations for becoming involved. When teachers "listen to" the voices of real youth it impossible to maintain the fiction that being young and gay is not difficult or even dangerous in today's culture.

I have found role-playing activities help students move from a psychology of the other to a phenomenology of the self (Sears 26). When individuals from majority groups virtually experience a small taste of the experiences of the minority they can grasp more clearly why the personal is indeed the political and the public/private dichotomy is broken down. For example, many students have commented on how enlightening "the pronoun game" has been for them in my class. At the beginning of one session I ask a few students to role-play a Monday morning teacher's lounge scenario in which one teacher attempts to keep private the gender of her or his date for the weekend while three other "curious" colleagues attempt to find out via a series of questions. The follow-up discussion reveals just how difficult it is to maintain one's sexual orientation as private knowledge and how straight people take it for granted that they can openly discuss their home lives in public. We address the notion of "special rights" by examining the ways homophobia and sexism work hand in hand to limit the choices of young people. When fear of being called a "fag" prevents an adolescent boy from pursuing artistic interests homophobia affects everyone in the culture. Each of these activities forces teachers to experience a little of why it is extremely unhealthy for young lesbians and gays to be forced to remain closeted and silenced by socializing institutions such as the school.

    The rhetoric of bureaucratic control is the most difficult to counter in the teacher education classroom. Even after teachers deconstruct the other arguments that exclude gays and lesbians from school discourse, they remain fearful of damaging their careers by asking their own students to participate in similar deconstructions. Regarding these fears, I have found it beneficial to bring in teachers who make their classes inclusive to serve as role models. I also encourage teachers to stop self-censoring themselves by at least asking their principals and curriculum coordinators how much support they could expect for making their curriculums more inclusive. We cannot know our own power until we attempt to exercise it. I also have found it is very important to make English teachers aware of all the support and resources they will have access to as members of their professional organizations and teacher unions. We review the resources made available for teachers facing censorship issues from The National Council of Teachers of English; The New York State English Council; The Southern Law Poverty Center; The Jewish Anti-Defamation League; The Gay, Lesbian, Straight Teachers Network; and the United Federation of Teachers. We discuss the empowerment teachers can achieve when we become active in our professional organizations as well as all of the resources and support available to us.

I do not want to pretend like the challenges of making our classes gay-friendly are not fraught with obstacles and real concerns. But I do know that change is possible and that educators working together can progress much farther than teachers working in isolation.

Works Cited

Fuoss, Kirk. "A Portrait of the Adolescent as a Young Gay: The Politics of Male Homosexuality in Young Adult Fiction." *Queer Words, Queer Images.* Ed. Jeffrey Ringer. New York: NYU Press, 1994.

Gee, James. *Sociolinguistics and Literacies.* London: The Falmer Press, 1990.

"GLSEN's 2001 school climate survey." 4 April 2002. <(http://www.glsen.org/templates/news/record.html)>.

Greenbaum, Nancy. "Literature Out of the Closet: Bringing Gay and Lesbian Texts and Subtexts Out in High School English." *English Journal.* 83(5), 71-74.

hooks, bell. *Teaching to Transgress.* New York: Routledge, 1994.

Linné, Rob. "Choosing Alternatives to 'The Well of Loneliness.'" *Thinking Queer: Sexuality, Culture, and Education.* Eds. Susan Talburt and Shirley Stienberg. New York: Peter Lang, 2000.

Merriam, Sharon. *Qualitative Research and Case Study Applications in Education.* Sacramento, CA: Jossey-Bass, 1997.

Pemberton-Butler, Lisa. "Teens Carry Diversity to Another Level with 'Safe Place' for Gays or Straights." *Seattle Times.* 16 October 2000.

Sears, James. "Thinking Critically, Intervening Effectively about Homophobia and Heterosexism." *Overcoming Heterosexism and Homophobia.* Eds. James Sears and Walter Williams. New York: Columbia University Press, 1997.

Sedgewick, Eve. "How to Bring Your Kids Up Gay." *Social Text*, 29 1991. 32-39.

Falseness cannot come from thee, for thou look'st
Modest as **Justice**, and thou seem'st a palace
For the crown'd truth to dwell in.

Pericles to Marina

In William Shakespeare's *Pericles*

V.i. 134-36

The Constructivist Classroom: An Antidote to Indifference

Laurie Iodice

"Indifference is not a beginning, it is an end. And, therefore, indifference is always the friend of the enemy, for it benefits the aggressor—never his victim, whose pain is magnified when he or she feels forgotten. The political prisoner in his cell, the hungry children, the homeless refugee—not to respond to their plight, not to relieve their solitude by offering a spark of hope is to exile them from human memory. And in denying their humanity we betray our own" (Wiesel 3).

Creating a classroom climate and curriculum that confront the millennial diseases of complacency and indifference is among the greatest challenges today's educators face. It is as great as safety concerns, fiscal dilemmas and testing worries, for without the development of empathy and discernment, current students who are our future shareholders in the democratic process will lack the affective and cognitive skills essential for continued development and refinement of the great national experiment—democracy. Though debates about values education have intervened intermittently since the beginning of compulsory public education in our country, we are operating under mythic delusions if we, as educators, believe that we are not part of the indoctrination process into social values. We participate in this process whenever we prepare students for standardized and statewide tests, when we invest in school-wide character education programs, and when we endorse zero-tolerance and other disciplinary policies. As English teachers, we more subtly influence when we purposefully foreground selected social and political values and draw attention away from others through reading selections and course inquiry topics and when we develop and model course practices that we value.

As a twenty-five year veteran of both the secondary and post-secondary English classroom, I have taught in a diocesan Catholic high school, a major university and two public high schools, and have experienced a wide variety of institutional values. Doing so has made me acutely conscious of each institution's impact on curricular decisions. When it comes to values education, we are all responsible, whether we participate consciously and willingly or not. Teaching and learning are both social acts. Jim Zebrosky implies this in his overview of the social constructivist psychologist, Lev Vygotsky, in *The Composition Chronicle* (1990).

> Lev Vygotsky, the Soviet psychologist and language theorist, long ago in the 1920s and 1930s worked through some of the intellectual consequences of seeing thinking in both social and individual terms. Vygotsky's psychology of process provides a possible corrective to views of writing that tend to see composition as either all social or all individual. In Vygotsky's psychology of process, the social is an intimate part of the development of the individual. In Mind in Society, Vygotsky argues that "human learning presupposes a specific social nature and a process by which children grow into the intellectual life of those around them."

The processes of thinking come out of the communities to which we belong; these processes are dynamic, constantly shifting, constantly being expanded and transformed. (4)

Teachers, too, grow out of their intellectual communities. Last term, when the district I teach for decided to give control of professional development to their teachers, they modeled the decentralized classroom. In their most recent professional development plan, teacher representatives and administrators selected six professional inquiry topics from which teachers would be able to choose when designing their personalized professional development plan for the year. The district provided release time for conferences and school visits, financial resources for books, for materials and for expert consultations, and allowed time during scheduled professional development days for teacher research, study groups and independent execution of professional goals related to the inquiry topic. It was synchronistic that the exploration into my selected topic, Constructivism, coincided with the opportunity to revise and to teach several sections of our school's tenth grade Interdisciplinary English/Social Studies honors course — an ideal forum for the constructivist approach.

Classrooms that center on just principles begin with teachers who are willing to relinquish the comfort of controlling their students' learning. Constructivism provides the theoretical framework for such practices. Several teachers in the high school English department gravitated toward this topic for their professional inquiry, perhaps because we intuitively recognized that many of our classroom methods were constructivist, in nature, but wished to acquire a language with which we might frame, reflect on, refine and articulate these practices. Constructivism promotes justice because it encourages a dialogic model. As indicated by Zebrosky during a Professional Development seminar, the implications of this dialogic model are numerous. According to Zebrosky, the dialogic model:

- allows theory to play a helpful role in teacher development by encouraging meta-cognitive practices.
- allows students to study and to learn from communities in which they are already involved or interested, so that reading and writing become both the subject of study and the means or instrument by which such learning takes place.
- views "process" not as a singular, linear, individual, official" series of steps. Instead, it views process as plural, uneven, layered, both social and individual.
- encourages holistic approaches to writing— the writing of whole pieces of discourse that one would likely encounter in the community.
- reaffirms the dangerous nature of tracking.
- sees writing as a reflection and refraction of social conflicts and antagonisms of a culture.
- questions our too easy categories of "author" and "text."
- encourages successful group work and one on one tutoring and conferencing as key sites for literacy development because they

encourage the interaction and internalization of dialogue into inner speech.
- foregrounds the notion that there is no "universal" literary process.
The differences across time and culture, then, become as important as the similarities.

The dialogic model allows theory to play a helpful role in teacher development by encouraging meta-cognitive practices. What the constructivist model allows for is a model of teaching that relies primarily on inquiry. This implies the willingness to relinquish control over daily class discussions and interactions, and to rely more heavily on what Cathy Fosnot labels, "the horizon" (Professional Development Seminar). "The horizon" is the long-range outcome goal we wish to meet by the end of a unit and/or a course. Developing one such goal in an inquiry model necessitates copious self-scrutiny, and ironically, careful planning. I confronted such scrutiny when I decided to entitle the soon-to-be revised interdisciplinary English course, "Perspectives on Human Nature," and to focus the course inquiry on a series of progressive questions upon which the course might pivot.

When I first designed the course in tandem with my Global History colleague, Anne Billings, I hoped to provide students opportunities for development of critical literacy practices in a holistic, integrated forum, one in which students would be able to discern the relationship between literacy issues and course texts in English and current events and historical trends in Global History. This ninth grade interdisciplinary course is grounded in the concept, *empathy*. In reviewing books that would enrich the revised Global History curriculum, Anne and I decided to build upon this notion of empathy by selecting *critical discernment* as the key underlying concept for our courses, as it seemed a natural outgrowth of the former. We define discernment as the ability to recognize, to assess and to accept the parameters and limits of personal, social, political, economic, cultural, literary and historical perspectives, including our own. In ninth grade, then, students engage in texts that would encourage awareness and sensitivity regarding a multiplicity of worldviews. In tenth grade, the cognitive move, then, becomes the move from awareness and sensitivity to objective assessment and critical judgment. What follows is the first page of the course syllabus; it outlines course goals, texts and the inquiry questions used to frame the term's exploration:

INTERDISCIPLINARY HONORS ENGLISH 10 PERSPECTIVES ON HUMAN NATURE

COURSE OVERVIEW:
Welcome to Interdisciplinary Honors English 10 – Perspectives on Human Nature.

Through our reading, writing and discussion this year, we will be exploring the human need for personal satisfaction—a recurring theme in literature. In ancient Greece, Socrates aptly referred to this as the search for "the good life." In the Middle Ages, Thomas Moore dubbed the ideal society as "utopia." During the Renaissance, Shakespeare, in The Tempest, coined the phrase "brave new world" to describe yet another utopian vision. More recently, culture critics such as Aldous Huxley and George Orwell, have taken a second look at the consequences of creating ideal societies. The question throughout history and literature remains—what is it specifically, that humans are searching for, and what is the relationship between what we are searching for, and what we (socially) create—between human nature and social realities—or culture? We will be exploring these and other questions through the world literature we read, discuss and write about this year. We will do so in connection to historical perspectives addressed in Global History, which focus on the relationships among nature, science and culture. Most specifically, we will explore the following questions:

What is "natural" in human nature?
What is the "nature" of human discontent and the need for change?
What are the benefits and costs of progress?
What is this concept we call "human rights?"
Why do some of us conform and others resist?
When (and in what ways) does the human spirit triumph and persist, despite adversity?
What role does language (in particular, written language) play in recording the human quest for the good life or the ideal society? In influencing it? In defining it?

REPRESENTATIVE TEXTS: The course includes such readings as:
Brief selections of fiction, nonfiction and poetry
Aldous Huxley, *Brave New World*
William Golding, *Lord of the Flies*
George Bernard Shaw, *Pygmalion*
William Shakespeare, *The Tempest*
Charlotte Perkins Gilman, *Herland*

George Orwell, *1984*
Eli Wiesel, *Night*
Art Spiegelman, *Maus I* and *Maus II*
Andre Brink, *A Dry White Season*
Choice books re: the theme of human rights and civil disobedience.
Cinematic texts such as *A Knight's Tale, Swing Kids, Night and Fog,* and *Pleasantville*

The course outline is a document I return to periodically throughout the year, as a vehicle for students and me to assess the course's recursive moves, as they relate to our growing awareness of the issues that emerge from our inquiry. Though my Social Studies partner and I meet regularly throughout the year to assess and to develop complementary course goals, what has transpired in our courses transcends our careful planning and is, in large part, due to the support of our colleagues and administrators and the intellectual willingness and engagement of our students.

The dialogic model allows students to study and to learn from communities in which they are already involved or interested, so that reading and writing become both the subject of study and the means or instrument by which such learning takes place. What is utopia? Students begin the year exploring this question through discussions of utopian poetry and through their collaborative designs and presentations of original utopias. Working in groups of four, they prepare a panel presentation illustrating and explaining their group's vision of the ideal society (utopia). Presentations must address the advantages and disadvantages of their selected features and must account for their choices, in light of potential drawbacks. Group members decide on all features together, but each group member is primarily responsible for presenting at least one feature from topics such as: the economic system, the government/political structure, the role of work and leisure, the education system, family structure and social values, and the role of technology.

After each presentation, student panelists field questions from class members. In addition, class scribes record an evolving list of presented utopian features. This student-generated list of values provides us with a benchmark for further inquiry. While students are presenting their utopian visions in class, they are concurrently reading Huxley's *Brave New World* at home. We introduce the first third of the novel early in the presentation planning stage, and students then complete the novel autonomously and record questions, reactions and impressions in a reader's log. The unit culminates with the development of a unit portfolio and their participation in an interdisciplinary town meeting that allows students to make connections across courses as they carefully consider complementary and competing views.

The portfolio is intended as a vehicle for demonstrating our students' understanding of the concepts we've read about and discussed, and for experimenting with these concepts, in terms of their own thinking and writing processes. Throughout the portfolio construction process, we are asking students to make connections, to assess preliminary data and to formulate a tentative hypothesis regarding the potential benefits and costs of progress. By doing so, they are essentially assessing the degree to which moving ahead may entail leaving others behind.

The dialogic model views "process not as a singular, linear, individual, official" series of steps. Instead, it views process as plural, uneven, layered, both social and individual. The culminating town meeting that takes place while students are designing their portfolios outside of class provides students the opportunity to further reflect on their learning experiences, to make connections, to question and to challenge. In Global History, they've written, thought about and discussed various eighteenth century philosophies concerning human "nature" –and have considered the degree to which humans might purposefully direct themselves toward improving their conditions. In English, they've attempted to design utopian communities that would enact their collective visions of what human improvement would look like and they have read a satirical portrait that cautions its readers about the possible price of attempting to improve the human condition through modern innovations. Their goal for the town meeting is to look for convergences and divergences among the many philosophies they have encountered. This sets in motion a recursive inquiry process in that we revisit initial views and confirm or revise them repeatedly throughout the year. The goal in doing so is to consistently provide students opportunities to not only engage in but to question and to reflect on literacy practices and their implications. The goal, as stated earlier, is discernment.

The dialogic model encourages holistic approaches to writing—the writing of whole pieces of discourse that one would likely encounter in the community. Following the opening unit, students continue inquiring into perspectives on human nature in the second unit which has as its central text, William Golding's *Lord of the Flies*. The unit exploration culminates in the ultimate classroom test of the justice system—the (mock) trial. In this case, it is an interdisciplinary trial modeled after Jim Burke's William Golding case (31). Here, students simulate an actual court case, trying William Golding for his views on human nature. As plaintiff, he becomes emblematic for the innate selfishness of humankind. Depending on their emerging views, students opt for defense or prosecution roles and collaborate with team members in preparing their case regarding human nature and selecting relevant historical and literary witnesses to testify in their favor.

As part of the process, students develop authentic court documents, which they present during the trial proceedings. They research their characters and their role responsibilities and attempt to adopt the voice of the figures they are portraying. The alternate section of Interdisciplinary English serves as jury for the Proceedings. It is the responsibility of each "jurist" to take notes and to write a concluding log that justifies his/her position, using evidence from the case to support claims. These are collected and tabulated, and after the head jurist declares a verdict, the judge prepares and delivers his statement for sentencing. Throughout the process, students not only come to appreciate the rhetorical goals and styles of various documents, but they begin to recognize both the benefits and the potential flaws of the justice system—even one grounded in democratic principles such as ours.

The dialogic model reaffirms the dangerous nature of tracking. There is a certain irony to the execution of this principle in that the course is tracked as an Honors course, yet one of its inquiry topics is the degree to which culture, and in particular, class shapes individual identity concepts. Through our reading and discussion of Pygmalion, in relation to a review of Social Darwinist theory in Global History, we raise such questions and explore them, even to the point of considering the course's "privileged" status among other course selections. Most specifically, we focus on issues of language, culture, manners, class and identity throughout the unit activities and discussions.

The dialogic model views writing as a reflection and refraction of social conflicts and antagonists of a culture. As the Global History course moves into its exploration into the topic, Colonialism, we begin our exploration of Shakespeare's, *The Tempest*, which provides opportunities for not only more conventional literary analysis, but both New Historical and Post-Colonial reconsiderations, as well. In the unit's culminating activity, students have an opportunity to commit themselves to a position, while recognizing its parameters and limitations. They do so in a panel style debate forum where they address such questions as the validity of determining social value based on dominant class standards, or the degree to which "upward mobility" is a legitimate class equalizer. They also consider the question of imperialism. When doing so, they debate whether we are doing more harm than good in holding "natives" accountable to Western standards of living and lifestyles. They also take into consideration the theories of Social Darwinists and post-colonial critics. Questions such as these prompt students to consider Western values within a broader context.

The dialogic model foregrounds the notion that there is no "universal" literary process. The differences across time and culture, then, become as important as the similarities. Language becomes the center of inquiry in our exploration of the next two course texts, *Herland* and *1984*. Both encourage an awareness of the social construction of knowledge and its possible price, in terms of limiting our personal constructions of self. In both units, students explore gendered language and politically correct language, through projects such as current events connections logs, the development of class lexicons and the partnered delivery of "double-think" speeches that encourage dualistic thinking. The goal here is to develop objectivity and the ability to delay judgment until ample data is accrued.

The dialogic model questions our too easy categories of "author" and "text." While reading such texts as Elie Wiesel's *Night* and Art Spiegalman's *Maus* series, during our Holocaust unit, students problematize notions of author and text when we consider memoir and oral history, as genres. We do so through crafting oral histories that require students to interview someone about a series of significant past events. Students then bear witness to this event by retelling it for the reader in a manner that they believe is logical and truthful. They are also expected to analyze their selection process. When restructuring and reordering their retelling of the story, for instance, students must address such decisions as: the choices they made about what to put in and what to leave out; the order in which they cast the information, and the occasions when they chose to use their subject's "exact" language, as well as the occasions when they used their own. Through their processes of interviewing and (re) constructing their subjects' stories, students encounter and account for the multiplicity of voices and texts involved — yet another move toward the development of discernment.

The dialogic model encourages successful group work and one on one tutoring and conferencing as key sites for literacy development because they encourage the interaction and internalization of dialogue into inner speech. Throughout the year, students regularly provide feedback for one another, both in terms of informal class interaction and more formalized written responses. They engage in writing practices such as dialogic journals, silent debates, cooperative class projects, rough draft peer workshops and editing sessions, and the development of class anthologies. They work with partners to develop and to deliver speeches; they regularly participate in "webbed" class discussions where they are required to actively listen and to comment on the last speaker's comments prior to providing their own responses. They also confer with me regarding evolving drafts, as needed. We also employ meta-cognitive practices such as writers' protocols and periodic self-assessments, as vehicles for further encouraging the development of critical judgment — a necessary prerequisite to the cultivation of a just social environment.

The dialogic process foregrounds the notion that there is no "universal" literary process. The differences across time and culture, then, become as important as the similarities. The course's final two units address the issue of justice more specifically, through students' inquiry into apartheid in Global History and their inquiry into Andre Brink's vision of apartheid in *A Dry White Season*, in English class. During the unit discussions, we address the issues raised in the novel, in relation to our growing awareness of our own sometimes competing, conflicting histories and present global circumstances. Once again, we take up the question of language, as it constructs, reveals and reflects our cultural awareness.

The course's final unit project involves a student-constructed variation of Tom Romano's multigenre paper that has as its focus of exploration the topic: Justice/Human Rights. Concurrently, students select a book from Amnesty's Human Rights Education Resource Notebook with the intention of integrating ideas from the choice work into their multi-genre papers. Students are expected to express a truth at the core of their paper, and it is up to them to decide just what this truth will be. Their analytic skills should be evidenced, though, by their ability to choose a truth based on critical judgment, complex thought and careful integration of secondary source ideas and information concerning the topic of justice as it relates to human rights:

> In a way, to be indifferent to suffering is what makes a human being inhuman. Indifference, after all, is more dangerous than anger and hatred. Anger can at times be creative. But

> indifference is never creative. Even hatred at times may elicit a response . . . Indifference elicits no response . . . Indifference is not a beginning; it is an end. (Wiesel 3)

The "end" in a constructivist classroom is antithetical to the one Wiesel cautions about. An inquiry-based course theoretically grounded in constructivist principles allows for an end to the miasma that is characteristic of students who are not actively engaged in their education. A just classroom is a classroom that enables students to construct meaning from their experiences and provides students with challenging, developmentally appropriate literacy practices from which they might write the world as an evolving text. It is a classroom that encourages responsive, creative, critical engagement with that world.

Works Cited

Burke, Jim. *The English Teacher's Companion*. Portsmouth: Boynton/Cook Publisher's Inc., 1999.

Fosnot, Cathy. Fayetteville-Manlius School District: Professional Development Seminar. 29 August 2001.

Romano, Tom. *Writing With Passion*. Portsmouth: Hienemann Press. 1995.

Wiesel, Elie. "The Perils of Indifference." The History Place: Great Speeches Collection. http://www.historyplace.com. 12 April 1999.

Zebrosky, James. "Constructivist Approaches in the Composition Classroom." Fayetteville-Manlius School District: Professional Development Seminar. 25 January 2002.

----------. "New Perspectives on the Social in Composition: Lev Vygotsky's Theory of Process." *Composition Chronicle*. April 1990.

In order to ensure a popular intelligence and an intelligent populace capable of democratic decision making, school must cultivate in all students the skills, knowledge, and understanding that both lead them to want to embrace the values undergirding our pluralistic democracy and arm them with a keen intelligence capable of free thought. Schools must provide an education that enables critical thinking *and* communal experience, so that citizens can intelligently debate competing ideas, weigh the individual and the common good, and make judgments that sustain democratic institutions and ideals.

Linda Darling-Hammond

"Education for Democracy"

Re-Viewing Multicultural Sites: An Inquiry of Transcultural Betweenness

Melissa Hasbrook

Knowledge emerges only through invention and re-invention, through the restless, impatient, continuing, hopeful inquiry human beings pursue in the world, with the world, and with each other. ~Paulo Freire, *Pedagogy of the Oppressed*

If multicultural education ever experienced criticism, today's scholars challenge its current versions from a range of fronts. Analyses expose sentimentalism, political correctness, and essentialist representations of racial experience to name only a few of the contested outcomes, as evidenced in its literature, curriculum, and theoretical frameworks. The difference multiculturalism made in education is much like the difference that Robert Frost's traveler in "The Road Not Taken" reflects upon: "Two roads diverged in a wood, and I--/ I took the one less traveled by, / And that has made all the difference." This poem—and particularly these lines—are used to motivate people to choose the road "less traveled by," assuming that this path offers something supposedly better. The traveler, though, reflects that the two roads "that morning equally lay," revealing that the difference made hasn't been necessarily more valuable but "just different." In light of current criticisms in multiculturalism, especially in terms of social justice, the feigned change resembles the traveler's perception of difference, something "just different," lacking the theoretical and practical bases to transform education toward an advocacy of equality.

Yet the venture of the multicultural is rooted in a reformatory project, one that pursued social equality initially in democratic education and now in what we typically recognize as the celebration of diversity. So, what happened in this pursuit of equality through education as seen in literature, paradigms for teaching, and the scholarship that influences these pedagogical outcomes? How did multiculturalism result in skin-deep changes? By exploring its historical legacy in democratic education and current discourses in multicultural scholarship, a recurring metanarrative of the Nation(al) surfaces, one promoting a nationalist project that uses individualism to achieve its ends. Hoffman challenges multicultural educators to become aware of the "culturally embedded, so that we may move toward a more self-aware multiculturalism with greater potential to inform practice" (546). An awareness of multiculturalism's development through this metanarrative of the Nation(al) and its persistence today makes possible breaking away from a nationalist path. In light of this historical development, forging new paths for social justice requires a transformative cultural inquiry that explores transcultural contexts. Inquiring transculturally in part means viewing cultural experience through rhetorical and relational dynamics, an inquiry that engages beliefs and actions.

Multiculturalism and Democratic Education: Partners in Time

We are in the middle of an extraordinary social experiment:
the attempt to provide education for all members of a vast pluralistic democracy. ~Mike Rose, *Lives on the Boundary*

Forging new paths involves deciding where our feet go, how the feet get there, what the mind envisions as a possible path, yet a reflection about *the path behind* — the events and contexts that lead to this moment of choice — should shape those outcomes. Multiculturalism is rooted in John Dewey's initial project of democratic education, a movement premised on nation building (Mitchell 2), as the United States shifted away from physical expansion through colonization to a focus on developing the nation's citizenry (3). Dewey's *Democracy and Education* was published originally in 1915 during the midst of World War I, in which he describes this time frame as one emphasizing "the idea of national sovereignty" (97) — or a nation's individual sovereignty amidst the international. The main premise that I encounter in Dewey's text is a proposal to mediate the individual and society, using education as the means of mediation through which a nation can shape its progress. By viewing, or "seeing", the international context in this way — a space or place "outside" of national borders, Dewey acknowledged an international dynamic of relationships. Yet he proposed that the reality of national sovereignty dictates that education operate within the context of the national, because educating students as international citizens would involve an oversized, decontextualized, unrealistic project (97). This mediation proposal was based upon a particular view of democratic life:

> A society which makes provision for participation in its good of all its members on equal terms and which secures flexible readjustment of its institutions through interaction of the different forms of associated

life is in so far democratic. Such a society must have a type of education which gives individuals a personal interest in social relationships and control, and the habits of mind which secure social changes without introducing disorder. (99)

A shared experience is key to what Dewey conceived to be "democratic." Control is emphasized before disorder, lending to a frame for social life and education that focuses upon the known elements of culture, excluding "the different." Dewey also emphasized individual responsibilities to the nation, a democracy that emphasized the civic citizen.

Focusing on the Nation(al) through a democratic frame, in part, embodied Dewey's advocacy of individual opportunity to escape class boundaries. He proposed that connecting individuals with the nation via education offered a way out or around class barriers, where education could function as an equalizer, and schools could operate as sites in which to mediate the individual and nation for particular goals. His goal for a version of individual opportunity achieved through education ultimately serves as a means by which to pursue national "progress." Dewey envisioned the individual as a potential creator of new knowledge in an educational context (296) as the means by which a nation advances itself (305). In fact, he viewed the creation of new knowledge to be a responsibility of the individual to the Nation by participating in its progress (295). Ironically, Dewey's framework valorizes individualism yet does so for the purpose of promoting nationalism.

In order to promote such national identity, Dewey advocated harmony for the sake of unity. As he linked progress with the improvement of "group habits" (79), his intent "to overcome" difference was not about confronting differences within educational sites. For example, addressing what to teach about "other nations," Dewey promoted a focus upon "commonalities" (98). Broadening students' perceptions by interacting with people was for the purpose of national progress within this way of "seeing" (123), not an understanding of and wrestling with difference. These strategies stem from a fear of social difference, as Dewey regarded social complexity to be dangerous (9), and hence his educational project aimed to develop "the habits of mind which secure social changes without introducing disorder" (99). In essence, this framework trained students to become blind to difference.[1]

Sociologist Craig Calhoun analyzes the rise of nationalism in Europe following the demise of communism, and offers relevant connections to the US context in light of Dewey's project, toward a motivation about why democratic education promotes the Nation(al):

> . . . individuals are directly members of the nation, that it marks each of them as an intrinsic identity and they commune with it immediately and as a whole. In ideology, at least, the individual does not require the mediations of family, community, region, or class to be a member of the nation. (396)

Dewey's proposal for education to mediate the individual with the nation also minimizes the role of other relationships, as individuals develop habits tying them to the nation. In Calhoun's view, individualism and the nation's strive toward "progress" are attempts to secure success amidst international competition (398). This pattern surfaces in Dewey's framework by promoting the narrative of the Nation in its progress, as this version of democratic education attempts by fixing identity and responsibility to individuals and their nation for international status.

Past Trends
In truth, we are neither only what we inherit nor only what we acquire but, instead, stem from the dynamic relationship between what we inherit and what we acquire. ~Paulo Freire, *Teachers as Cultural Workers*

Dewey's initial democratic project widened under the pressures of cultural pluralism in the 1940s, as the US public confronted the racial segregation and disenfranchisement—"legally, economically, and culturally"—of primarily African Americans (Mitchell 4). Regarding this historical moment, May's review on versions of multicultural education in the US exposes efforts to resolve "the 'ethnic minority' crisis" (*Critical Multiculturalism* 32), a point of view holding that

> Minority groups should be absorbed into that nation's "culture" (i.e. the culture of the dominant group) as quickly as possible in order to be able to contribute fully to the creation and maintenance of society. Conversely, maintaining ethnic minority language(s) and culture(s) is seen as a direct threat to the stability of society. (33)

The extension of the democratic project to resolve inequalities by equalizing individual opportunity moved "beyond" class to race. In other words, initially democratic education recognized class status as a potential obstacle to individual opportunity and came to regard racial status in the same way. With these analyses, multicultural democratic education recruited citizens from certain class and racial statuses to participate in the narrative of Nation(al) progress, aiming to resolve the perception of an "ethnic crisis."

The failure of this mediation between individual citizens of such backgrounds within the nation unraveled with US racial tensions of the 1960s and 1970s (Mitchell 10). At this point, an open admissions policy in postsecondary institutions led to an influx of minority students. Many of these students challenged the limited range of perspectives addressed in English studies (Rodriguez *Hunger* 157). Archives from the Universities of Michigan and Washington document teacher and student interactions based on perceptions about race, stemming from a "concern for minority education" by composition and literature faculty (Barnett 15). A graduate student during the time, author Richard Rodriguez attributes the development of ethnic studies as a reaction to these students' concerns (*Hunger* 157). Apparently, the challenge to a canon with a particular kind of literature prompted educators and educational institutions to change, leading to the development of multicultural literature.

On the surface, the institutional and literary changes appear to be significant, with programs like Latino and African American studies at universities and never ending publications categorized as multicultural literature. Looking more carefully, though, as the traveler reflects in "The Road Not Taken," these differences are "skin-deep."

When considering the curriculum trends for multiculturalism and to understand this skin-deep change, collective identity is important to consider. Pluralism and the Civil Rights Movement pressed for collective identities within the nation, pressures that challenged nationalistic individualism. When the basis of citizenship rights is individually based, tensions surface as groups advocate for "differentiated citizenship" (Kymlicka 174). By nature of their resistance to this status quo position on citizenship rights in the US, such group members became candidates, or targets, for mediation in order to protect the perception of Nation(al) unity. For example, Rodriguez received many offers as a prospective doctoral graduate because of his *perceived* Chicano status, positions that he turned down in the midst of conflicted feelings towards the advantaged status he earned because of the image others maintained about him (*Hunger* 171). In these ways, the emphases on shared life experience and civic-ness, prominent in Dewey's initial version of democratic education, were promoted.

Present Trends
If the subaltern cannot speak, it is only because the scholar cannot listen and hear. ~Ellen Cushman, The Struggle and The Tools

Politically charged moves to select recruiting perceived ethnic representatives reflect curriculum changes bearing the label of multicultural. Celebrating the individual is a trend that creates cookie-cutter versions of cultural experience (Hoffman 558) and is situated in a broader critique of decontextualized explorations within multicultural education (Nieto 206). Ironically, Dewey sought a "realistic" context through emphasizing the Nation(al), but today's multiculturalism fails to offer adequate, if any, context for cultural inquiry. This individualistic version frames cultural difference merely as a matter of personality, some "thing" of equal difference on an individual basis. Scholar of Native American studies LeBeau critiques representations of Indians on the basis of their individualism as a misrepresentation or distortion because of a failure to recognize, and inquire about, their lives and experiences as community members and advocates. For example, this trend is noted easily when scanning titles of biographies on such figures. His critique applies to my teaching context for a 200-level required arts and humanities course, in which materials and syllabus guidelines focused upon individual historical figures, like Frederick Douglass and Martin Luther King, Jr. Both of these instances expose a curriculum focus that separates individuals from communities that potentially could complete with a promotion of the Nation(al).

Calhoun's examination of nationalism offers an insight to this pattern: "In the formative phases of nationalism, heroic *individuals*—cultural as well as military and political heroes—figure prominently, but often in the established nation, *conformity* to the common culture becomes a central value" [emphasis added] (397). In the US, some individuals selected as historical and cultural figures have conformed to the common culture, or are re-presented, or remembered, in this unified way. For example, US attitudes towards King after he was assassinated pegged him as peaceful, contrasting popular perceptions about Malcolm X as violent. Yet what is overlooked, or made "invisible," in this re-presenting are the aggressive attitudes towards King prior to his assassination,[2] and Malcolm X's radical change toward the possibility of racial reconciliation without violence (341). Individualizing collective identities in these ways constitutes a selection process that deems certain persona as representatives for a cultural group that leads to these cookie-cutter categories, similar to a process of authenticating authors in multicultural literature.[3] Calhoun analyzes that the nationalistic state encourages an "increasing reliance on categorical identities rather than webs of relational identities" (398). Responses to the pluralistic and Civil Rights movements demonstrate this categorical reliance, akin to Dewey's approach to focus on commonalities, rather than dealing with differences. These trends reflect a universalistic assumption that does not value or esteem one's origins or heritage as relevant to one's present and future (May *Multicultural Education* 3). Consequently, the metanarrative of the Nation(al) created and maintains multiculturalism as a mold for singular or one-dimensional casts of culture, ultimately an essentialist project in shaping nationalistic identity.

This metanarrative of the Nation(al) resurfaces in the discourse of today's scholarship on multiculturalism, specifically addressing the development of a national citizenry in education, much like Dewey's initial project of democratic education. Both Nieto and Sleeter assess that skeptics—or conservative critics—view multiculturalism as destructive to this development, while advocates—or radical critics—view multiculturalism as potentially constructive. Of particular interest in this democratic discourse are advocates whose reviews on multiculturalism exemplify the persistence of this metanarrative in light of

Calhoun's analysis about "cultural and social factors [that] have converged to create and disseminate the notion of national identity" — individualism (396) and the state or nation (397).

In her review of "anthropological critiques of contemporary American multiculturalism" (545), Hoffman problematizes the ways in which self-esteem discourse in multiculturalism emphasizes the individual before the collective on the basis that such an emphasis does not necessarily apply "cross-culturally" (560), a criticism which she is unable to escape. By cautioning that "a view of self-esteem based on this sense of uniqueness may be accurate for *Americans* but not necessarily in *other cultural contexts*" [emphasis added] (560), she flattens identity and culture one dimensionally on the basis of nationality. She distinguishes "American" from "other cultural contexts" while appealing to the context of "cross-cultural," exposing a fixed perception of national borders. Hoffman's move to make space for "different" identities simultaneously essentializes "American," demonstrating the categorical tokenizing prevalent in multiculturalism today through a metanarrative of the Nation(al) that distinguishes Americans on the basis of individualism. This discourse reflects Dewey's initial project in fixing a connection between individuals and the nation through the mediation of education.

In a different instance, Sleeter dismisses certain scholarship from her review of critiques on multiculturalism, such as British work, on a certain premise: "Lively debates rage in other countries about multicultural education . . . but although issues overlap, they do not cross *national borders* cleanly enough to include in this review in a concise and coherent manner" [emphasis added] (81). Later in her review, Sleeter objects to multiculturalism critics who draw upon British antiracist scholarship and ignore work on race by US scholars of color (90). This criticism reveals another layer *within* Sleeter's categorization of scholarship, motivated by maintaining the fixedness of national borders. Her rhetoric reveals a rigid concept of borders, in light of her comments on scholars who privilege work not just by race but also by nationality. Another reflection about this discourse pattern points to nationalistic practice in response to racist practice.

The rhetoric of scholarly talk on the multicultural takes form within educational institutions, as earlier examined in curriculum trends and experiences like Rodriguez's. Research by Katharyne Mitchell on interactions between a school system and an immigrant community in Canadian British Columbia is framed in the historical context of Dewey's project in partnership with multicultural education. Educators rejected efforts of parents from this community to challenge particular practices, including hands-on activities and minimal homework--practices that educators viewed to respect student individuality (12). Although educators met face-to-face with parents, the requested changes were rejected under the guise of upholding multiculturalism (13). Mitchell links this instance of educators' inflexibility with the nationalistic agenda in multiculturalism (15), an instance uncovering citizens that promote a brand of individualistic nationalist multiculturalism that fails to reinvent itself in a context of multicultural relationships. In such cases, the educational institution serving as a site of mediation in which the metanarrative of the Nation(al) is told through the tool of multiculturalism. The sabotage of immigrants' resistance offers a parallel to the way in which racial minorities' attempts to reform English studies during the Civil Rights Movement were appropriated—through a privileging of individualism.

While these reviews address valid problems needing attention to transform the multicultural, the scholars exhibit exclusionary patterns that Mitchell links with a nationalistic agenda, making visible how Sleeter sets sites toward this agenda and Hoffman demonstrates its blind pursuit. Each similarly excludes voices or perspectives, which multiculturalism (cl)aims to include or "see." Ironically, Sleeter points out that conservative critics label multicultural inquiry as "un-American" (90) and attempt to create a picture of "the ugly multiculturalist:" "a frenzied mob of anti-Americans trying to destroy the United States, joined by 'ugly' feminists and Third World immigrants, and led by angry African American men of weak intellect" (89). Such tactics appeal to the nationalistic individualism that Calhoun analyzes.

Gauging New Sites: In Between
I was curious as I watched Cecilia take up guitar lessons
if she would ever find the truly in-between space that might settle her disquiet, something that would break from hip hop/heart throb and yet embrace something Latino/a while simultaneously breaking from alternative music and yet embracing something white. ~Ralph Cintron, *Angels' Town*

Excluding voices along national borders demonstrates an inability to recognize the transcultural—a site amidst today's globalization in which identity is multi-layered, intersecting, and changing, in which complex differences exist between individuals within any community, in which people identify with more than one nation or culture. Part of the difficulty interrogating the transcultural is the international competition in which nationalism operates, which lends to a policing of national borders in education that intentionally or blindly fails to inquire culture as an exploration of transcultural experiences and identities. Critical cultural inquiry requires redefining "the very concepts of homogeneous national cultures" toward a "'new' internationalism . . . that does not totalize experience," as Homi Bhabha proposes in today's "post-modern condition" (5). He positions this new internationalism in the local, the everyday transactions of our lives—"a local or transnational reality" (6). Mitchell also uses the term "transnational" in her research with the British Colombian immigrant community who valued certain educational practices after moving to Canada and continuing previous connections from Hong Kong, pointing to transnational as an experience of betweenness and multiplicity. For example, Bhabha explains a change facing Western nations, like Canada from Mitchell's research and the US from Sleeter's review of critiques: "The Western metropole must confront its postcolonial history, told by its influx of postwar migrants and refugees, as an indigenous and native narrative *internal to its national identity*" [emphasis his] (6). This sense of identity reveals the multi-layered and intersecting reality (or realities) of people living in a co-constructed and dynamic nation. It also offers reason why Sleeter's attempts to bound scholarship by nationality is artificial, since the students and communities for which multiculturalism (cl)aims to advocate live within various boundaries at different times and whose experiences and identities traverse between Hoffman's "American" and "other."

Bhabha also uses the term "translational," a kind of writing that surfaces as people negotiate values promoted within the national (or dominant) culture. These negotiations take place in sites of betweenness—the intersections experienced by the immigrants that Mitchell describes. Bhabha proposes that these sites are between the pedagogical and performative:

> In the production of the nation as narration there is a split between the continuist accumulative temporality of the pedagogical, and the repetitious, recursive strategy of the performative. It is through this process of splitting that the conceptual ambivalence of modern society becomes the site of *writing the nation*. (145)

He highlights the paradox that (re)telling the metanarrative of the Nation(al) creates between the pedagogical—the instructional, the *Bildung*, the project attempted by nationalistic agendas—and the performative—the lived experience, everyday actions that resist carrying out the pedagogical. Bhabha names this mismatch as a "process of splitting," one in which there is possibility "to reinscribe our human commonality" (7) as "writing the nation" takes place in this site of splitting. He describes this between space as liminal, comparing the space to a pathway or stairwell (4). In this sense, Bhabha locates culture as experiential, continually (re)created, viewing people as sites of on-going negotiation. By doing this, he challenges

an illusory agency that subscribers of the Nation(al) metanarrative privilege:
> The liminality of the people--their double-inscription as pedagogical objects and performative subject--demands a 'time' of narrative that is disavowed in the discourse of historicism where narrative is only the agency of the event, or the medium of a naturalistic continuity of Community or Tradition. (151)

Liminality—betweenness, the site within or between the pedagogical and performative—makes possible the agency to write culture differently, which Bhabha describes as occurring through "the process of dissemination—*of* meaning, time, peoples, cultural boundaries and historical traditions" (166). This trans, or liminal, space demands a version of democratic education contextualized inter- (and intra-) nationally that relinquishes the historical trend of emphasizing shared lived experience, pressing to explore the unknown, unlike popular versions of difference in multiculturalism.

Exposing the metanarrative of the Nation(al) calls for understanding right now how "nationalism is all too often the enemy of democracy rooted in civil society" (Calhoun 404). Part of this understanding must confront the nationalist surges in today's war-minded context, eerily considered by Calhoun nearly a decade ago:
> Although national identity may be a source of inspiration or national pride, or of a sense of obligation to help others by pursuing the common good of the United States ahead of the general good of humanity, it is unlikely to

be an identity which "trumps" all others. Of course, it is an open question how long this would last if the United States ever came under sever external pressure, or wars were again fought on American soil. Nationalism comes to the fore under a variety of historically specific circumstances—like war—as well as perhaps being comparatively stronger in some cultural traditions than others. (403)

Transforming intentional or blind nationalism into a site of visible transculturalism involves unmasking celebratory versions of multiculturalism as a celebration of the Nation(al) with a democratic guise. Rather than avoiding potential conflicts stemming from confronting discrimination or Western biases, in turn promoting a singular and static concepts of culture and the citizen, we must reinvent the multicultural by exploring transcultural experiences in rhetorical and relational ways. In order to shape a theoretical framework for on-going reinvention, the assumed essentialism of collective identity must be revised. Revising such essentialist assumption means that we must move beyond popular multiculturalism's carefree stroll through a tokenized version of culture that resembles Disney's Epcot Center, in which selected nations are represented with particular sites that cater to a stereotypical perspective of culture, complete with employees recruited from that nation. Transforming these Epcot-nation ideas of the multicultural requires breaking down attempts to colonize identity in national terms.

As Bhabha suggests, challenging a homogenous sense of nationality requires acknowledging the complex cultural experience of people's shifting connections to various identities, including legitimate connections to particular communities beyond the nation. By breaking out of this nationalistic pattern, Epcot multiculturalism would not need to employ rigid criteria for so-called representatives from a particular nation or culture, as typically happens when curriculum fixes author authenticity in multicultural literature. With experiences such as Rodriguez's, in which someone is perceived as ethnic (i.e. Chicano) while the person does not identity with that cultural experience, s/he may associate more closely with a cultural experience (i.e. white middle-classness) that contradicts those faulty perceptions. While Rodriguez is visible as an author, people have misread him intentionally or blindly to his transcultural experiences and are unwilling or unable to see his sites. For Rodriguez, visibility as a writer places him in a certain anthologies and shelves of bookstores (Latino), an error in location from his view (Brown 26). Moving to a transcultural site then makes visible complexities, including such contradictions in perceptions.

Exploring collective identity in its complexity of varied experiences (i.e. persons *assumed* to be a member of a cultural community) also involves confronting the postmodern critique that typically faults collective identity as necessarily essentialist in the midst of Epcot multiculturalism. May (*Critical Multiculturalism*) and Appiah both critique the essentializing assumption of scholars who dismiss the legitimacy of collective identity on the basis that they are necessarily essentialist.

> It would be too large a claim that the identities that claim recognition in the

multicultural chorus *must* be essentialist and monological. But it seems to me that one reasonable suspicion of much contemporary multicultural talk is that is presupposes conceptions of collective identity that are remarkably unsubtle in their understandings of the processes by which identities, both individual and collective, develop. (Appiah 156)

What is critiqued in light of Bhabha's discussion is the pedagogical stance of persons advocating the nationalistic project. Such a position "presupposes conceptions of collective identity," overlooking the performative of people's everyday and complex cultural experience, as well as sites of betweenness—liminality of people or "the processes by which identities . . . develop." Views that *prescribe* a "necessarily essentialist" assumption about collective identity fail to critically explore the range of possible cultural experiences that includes group identities.

Cognizance of these limitations in approaching multicultural inquiry (the automatic categorization of someone's culture based on appearance or parentage, rejecting the legitimate possibility for collective identity, etc.) requires exploring the complexities that exist between binaries that are result in perceptions of "either-or," like American vs. Other. Considering these between places and spaces, conceptualizations about identity and nationality will transform singular notions of cultural experience through challenging cultural assumptions. A critical inquiry of culture that explores sites of betweenness—the dialectic between the pedagogical and performative—involves exploring relationships linking people from various sites of betweenness and the discourses used as they negotiate interactions, thereby attempting to make vision possible, or to bring visibility, to ignored or unseen cultural experiences. This kind of critical inquiry must be transcultural in light of our contemporary context of globalization requiring awareness, respect, and understanding of cultural identifications that include more than one nation or culture.

By interrogating such transcultural relationships, social structures or systems are explored, including the range of identity factors—not only culture in terms of nationality or race. Our interactions within the classroom, such as moments of conflict between students, are an integral part of such critical inquiry, as well as self-reflexivity on the part of educators to examine our teaching practices related to the multicultural. The rhetorical patterns of discourse and their significance offer possibilities for such inquiry, as Keith Gilyard effectively proposes:

> If the ascension toward a more perfect democracy depends upon citizens being able to interrogate and resist *discourses* that impede such instantiation, as I suggest is the case, then students need to comprehend as completely as possible how discourse operates, which means understanding how the dominant or most powerful discourse serves to regulate and reproduce patterns of privilege . . . In short, students will need to engage in discussions of culture, ideology, hegemony, and asymmetrical power *relations*—all that rugged theoretical terrain

that sometimes seems far removed from the texts they are generating in *seemingly smooth sites.* [emphasis added] (266) Gilyard describes democracy as something that can be improved—"a more perfect democracy," in which citizens strive to understand and challenge barriers to the development of a more just society. How does this version of democracy differ from Dewey's initial project in democratic education? When Gilyard speaks of "democratic citizens," he contextualizes his proposal in "the trans:" "If we agree to aim for a radical *transcultural* democracy, . . . then we need pedagogies to foster the development of the critical and astute citizenry that would pursue the task" [emphasis added] (262). This emphasis contrasts Dewey's choice to develop citizens for the nation's progress within a competitive international context. Gilyard, and scholars like Bhabha, May, and Mitchell, promote critical cultural inquiry in terms of a democratic world in which social justice is advocated for humanity. The scope of this discussion doesn't offer the opportunity to explore the implications of globalization, yet this intensifying trend presses us to rethink what has been regarded historically as national sovereignty in particular terms: "The body politic can no longer contemplate the nation's health as simply a civic virtue; it must rethink the question of rights for the entire national, and international, community" (Bhabha 6).

Critical Cultural Inquiry: A Transformative Framework
What seems needed is not multicultural education as a set of techniques or discrete factual content, but as a process of critical

engagement — with self, others, texts, and ideas . . . ~Susan Florio-Ruane, *Teacher Education and the Cultural Imagination*

From Gilyard's overarching but particular description, how do we translate these goals into practice as we attempt to inquiry cultural experience critically, in nonessentialist ways that are cognizant of the transcultural, relational, and rhetorical? Calhoun offers a starting point for this kind of inquiry:

> The issue is *not just whether* people are members of one or another nation, *or whether* a particular claimed nation has the right to self-determination, but [1a] *what it means* to be a member of that nation, [2a] *how* it is to be understood, and [3a] *how it relates* to the other identities its members may also claim or be ascribed. [emphasis added] (394)

Green and Pearlman offer a parallel perspective in their review of multicultural education that advocates moving "away from notions of nationalism" (18):

> The perceived educational crisis is not just the result of a gap in knowledge but gaps in culture and how people learn. It is based on [1b] differences in viewpoint, [2b] how that viewpoint is communicated and [3b] how people interact. (22)

Calhoun's perspective on nationality interestingly intersects with Green and Pearlman's perspective on an *assumed* crisis in multicultural education in significant ways. Calhoun emphasizes exploring meaning making [1a] — who's involved, what forces dominate, why certain definitions are shaped. Green and Pearlman's acknowledgment of differing perspectives [1b] connects with meaning making, because various cultural experiences result in varied concepts of community membership. For example, some people assume that a cultural association is based on heritage while others on experience (i.e. Rodriguez's experiences). Calhoun considers ways in which such meanings are "understood" [2a], partly one's way of making meaning and also the delivery of such meanings by others, such as the presentation of certain ideas as facts or attempts of persuasion to influence people's understanding (i.e. rhetoric promoting nationalistic progress). In this way, understanding meaning corresponds to communication about that meaning, or viewpoint, as Green and Pearlman indicate [2b]. From these springboards—meaning-making and understanding its processes and consequences—possibilities arise to challenge perspectives that fail to capture the complexities of culture in its relationships [3a] or interactions [3b]. In order to deliberate cultural meanings, and what influences shape meaning-making, relationships must be deliberated within, or between, the complexities of cultural experiences.

A point-by-point framework within which these springboards fit is Nieto's proposal to reinvent multicultural education, a version that:
[a] "affirms students' culture without trivializing the concept of culture itself,"
[b] "challenges hegemonic knowledge" (206),
[c] "complicates pedagogy" (207),
[d] "problematizes a simplistic focus on self-esteem" (208), and
[e] "encourages 'dangerous discourses'"

--a framework which "by itself cannot do it all" (209). From this discussion, a transformative theoretical framework for the multicultural embraces collective identity without essentializing it [a], exposes and resists a metanarrative of the Nation(al) [b], confronts difference in all its messiness with the risk of conflict [d], and creates new discourses to explore the transcultural [e]. Nieto focuses on "the complex interplay of relationships within families, communities, and schools" (205) for implementing this plan. With Calhoun, Green and Pearlman, and Nieto's points in mind, practical approaches to critical cultural inquiry can operate in a framework that interrogates interactions as sites of on-going negotiation amidst intersecting identities and interactions.

The intentional or blind (re)telling of the metanarrative of the Nation(al) in multicultural scholarship reveals the complications stemming from pedagogy addressed by Nieto [c], complications also addressed by Ajay Heble. From examining his experiences teaching a "full year 200 [honors] level seminar in English" (149), Heble advocates an interventionist approach when discrimination surfaces in class discussions, positing intervention as ethical pedagogy. He faults "institutionalized notions of individualism" (151) as the basis for his students' division, reminiscent of outcomes from Dewey's initial democratic project and its long-term partnership with multiculturalism. Heble's questions are useful for forging new paths in multicultural democratic education toward social justice:

> Specifically, how do we reconcile our responsibility, as teachers, to ensure that teaching and learning are . . . sites of

obligation and loci of ethical practices . . . with a commitment to *democratizing* the classroom, to creating *participatory* spaces for the shaping and production of knowledge . . . ? What strategies can we develop that would enable us to *negotiate in* the classroom *between* our desire to promote free speech and the ethical imperative to prevent hate speech? [emphasis added] (147)

What Heble calls "participatory spaces" — spaces in which students as well as teachers "negotiate" — is akin to Bhabha's liminal space. "Participation," as Heble describes, results from an exchange between the pedagogical and performative, resulting in knowledge. This knowledge, though, isn't attributed solely to the individual for the purpose of national progress, but toward "democratizing the classroom" for socially just ways of interacting in classrooms.

The scholarship examined throughout this discussion advocates a sharp turn away from "doing diverse literature" (Heble 154), and admitting that we do not know how to "do multiculturalism" (Hoffman 565). Alternatively, in critical cultural inquiry, we must focus on "the way" we teach (Nieto 207). From this position, we can approach literature and composition by exploring the in-between sites that Bhabha describes. Hoffman proposes that educators need to

> be open to a pedagogy that challenges self-complacency and recognizes alternative visions of self . . . [to pursue] the oft-stated goals of empowerment for social action, for, unless the American cultural bias toward

> valuing the self at the expense of collectively is put into question, empowerment is mainly another word for the unquestioned dominance of an individualism that oppresses. (562)

In light of the legacy of early democratic education, a key challenge in making a difference in multicultural education—in its literature and pedagogy—is to develop a critical eye. This way of seeing reminds one's self about the ingrained tendency to (re)tell the metanarrative of the Nation(al) while catalyzes action toward social justice. In Paulo Freire's words, "This discovery cannot be purely intellectual but must involve action; nor can it be limited to mere activism, but must include serious reflection: only then will it be a praxis" (65).

[1] While immigration is not addressed in this text by Dewey, the US of 1915 was in the midst of a rising anti-immigrant sentiment (Decker; Nowlin). In 1925, the Immigrant Act was passed, severely capping immigration to the US. Amidst foreign policy and these domestic events, Dewey's project would aim to discount difference brought to the classrooms for the purpose of maintaining order.

[2] Professor of History Tom Summerhill's personal communication.

[3] Cai and Bishop in "Multicultural Literature for Children" demonstrate this process of author authenticity based on race, much akin to the problematic perceptions about identity that Rodriguez continues to challenge today (Brown).

The author wishes to thank Diane DuBose Brunner and Susan Florio-Ruanne who read the manuscript and made helpful comments.

Works Cited

Appiah, K. Anthony. "Identity, Authenticity, Survival: Multicultural Societies and Social Reproduction." *Multiculturalism: Examining the Politics of Recognition.* Ed. Amy Gutmann. Princeton, NJ: Princeton UP, 1994. 149-63.

Barnett, Timothy. "Reading 'Whiteness' in English Studies." *College English* 63.3 (2000): 9-37.

Bhabha, Homi K. *The Location of Culture.* 1994. London: Routledge, 1998.

Cai, Mingshui, and Rudine Sims Bishop. "Multicultural Literature for Children: Towards a Clarification of the Concept." *The Need for Story: Cultural Diversity in Classroom and Community.* Ed. Anne Haas Dyson and Celia Genishi. USA: NCTE, 1994. 57-71.

Calhoun, Craig. "Nationalism and Civil Society: Democracy, Diversity, and Self-Determination." *International Sociology* 8.4 (1993): 387-411.

Decker, Jeffrey Louis. "Corruption and Anti-Immigrant Sentiments Skew a Traditional American Tale." *Readings on* The Great Gatsby. Ed. Katie DeKoster. San Diego: Greenhaven Press, 1998. 121-32.

Dewey, John. *Democracy and Education*. 1915. New York: The Free Press, 1966.

Freire, Paulo. *Pedagogy of the Oppressed*. 1970. New York: The Continuum International Publishing Group Inc., 2000.

Gilyard, Keith. "Literacy, Identity, Imagination, Flight." *CCC* 52.2 (2000): 260-72.

Green, Stanton W. and Stephen Pearlman. "Putting the Culture into Multicultural Education: Toward a Critical Model of Cultural Literacy." *Interdisciplinary Curricula, General Education, and Liberal Learning: Selected Papers from the Annual Conference of the Institute for the Study of Post-secondary Pedagogy 1993*. Ed. Richard Kelder. ERIC. 1994. 18-29.

Heble, Ajay. "Re-ethicizing the Classroom: Pedagogy, the Public Sphere, and the Postcolonial Condition." *College Literature* 29.1 (2002): 143-60.

Hoffman, Diane M. "Culture and Self in Multicultural Education: Reflections on Discourse, Text, and Practice." *American Educational Research Journal* 33.3 (1996): 545-69.

Kymlicka, Will. *Multicultural Citizenship: A Liberal Theory of Minority Rights.* Oxford: Clarendon Press, 1995.

Malcolm X. *The Autobiography of Malcolm X.* 1964. USA: Grove Press, Inc., 1992.

May, Stephen. "Critical Multiculturalism and Cultural Difference: Avoiding Essentialism." *Critical Multiculturalism: Rethinking Multicultural and Antiracist Education.* Ed. Stephen May. London: Falmer Press, 1999. 11-41.

----------. "Multicultural Education and Rhetoric of Pluralism." *Making Multicultural Education Work.* Ed. Stephen May. England: Multilingual Matters, 1994. 32-47.

Mitchell, Katharyne. "Education for Democratic Citizenship: Transnationalism, Multiculturalism, and the Limits of Liberalism." *Harvard Educational Review* 71.1 (2001). <http://113868:harvard@www.edreview.org/harvard01/2001/p01/p01mitch.htm>.

Nieto, Sonia. "Critical Multicultural Education and Students' Perspectives." *Critical Multiculturalism: Rethinking Multicultural and Antiracist Education.* Ed. Stephen May. London: Falmer, 1999. 191-215.

Nowlin, Michael. "F. Scott Fitzgerald's Elite Syncopations: The Racial Make-up of the Entertainer in the Early Fiction." *English Studies of Canada* 26 (2000): 409-43.

Rodriguez, Richard. "Brown." *The American Scholar* 71.2 (2002): 13-29.

----------. *Hunger of Memory: The Education of Richard Rodriguez.* 1982. New York: Bantam Books, 1983.

Sleeter, Christine E. "An Analysis of the Critiques of Multicultural Education." *Handbook of Research on Multicultural Education.* Ed. James A. Banks. New York: Macmillan Pub, 1995. 81-94.

As I have understood it and experienced it myself, world literature is no longer an abstraction or a generalized concept invented by literary critics, but a common body and common spirit, a living, heartfelt unity reflecting the growing spiritual unity of mankind. State borders still turn crimson, heated red-hot by electric fences and machine-gun fire; some ministries of internal affairs still suppose that literature is "an internal affair" of the countries under their jurisdiction; and newspaper headlines still herald, "They have no right to interfere in our internal affairs!" Meanwhile, no such thing as INTERNAL AFFAIRS remains on our crowded Earth. Mankind's salvation lies exclusively in everyone's making everything his business, in the people of the East being anything but indifferent to what is thought in the West, and in the people of the West being anything but indifferent to what happens in the East. Literature, one of the most sensitive and responsive tools of human existence, has been the first to pick up, adopt, and assimilate this sense of the growing unity of mankind. I therefore confidently turn to the world literature of the present, to hundreds of friends whom I have not met face to face and perhaps never will see.

My friends! Let us be helpful, if we are worth anything.

Alexander Solzhenitsyn

"The One Great Heart"

Promoting Social Justice in the Young Adult Literature Class: Preparing Pre-Service Teachers to Choose Multicultural Texts

Alice L. Trupe

In recent years, we have been shocked by violent eruptions of adolescent rage that take the lives of schoolchildren and by brutal beatings or simple harassment of those who are "different," demonstrating our society's continuing intolerance in the face of demographic changes that guarantee "difference" will be the norm in the United States in the twenty-first century. Reports on school violence have repeatedly identified intolerance or ostracism as a factor in triggering shooting sprees. Media debates over racial profiling follow in the wake of violent incidents, whether crime in the local community or terrorism on the global level. In a climate of distrust, the challenge of literacy instruction is to foster empathy and imaginative identification with other human beings, no matter what their racial, ethnic, religious, or gender identity.

Many arguments for expanding the literary canon to include texts from a wide range of cultures have been advanced and widely accepted, and students at most colleges and universities enjoy a new range of literature courses that were not available twenty-five years ago. Not only may they choose courses in South African Literature, Native American Literature, or Asian-American Literature, it is likely that any survey or introductory literature course they take will include texts from a range of cultures. The multicultural curriculum is well established at the elementary level as well. Today, children begin their careers in literacy with stories about Anansi and Iktomi, and they are likely to read texts by Chinua Achebe, Maya Angelou, Toni Morrison, and Alice Walker in college classes.

Yet a gap in multicultural reading often occurs in the curriculum for "young adult" readers—a group with flexible boundaries defined by age and, consequently, interests, on the one hand, and by reading level, on the other. Children in middle school and high school often go directly from reading a range of children's literature to reading from the historical canon, a curricular invention solidly established at the end of the nineteenth century, as Arthur Applebee has shown. The canon may change over time, but the *idea* of the canon as necessary cultural knowledge remains firmly fixed. Many canonical works are difficult for adolescents to read and may not seem to have much relevance to their immediate experience. Outside of school, young readers' personal tastes may take them to series books, many of which are set in a generic middle-class culture in which various adventures involve mostly white, middle-class children. Many students who have read avidly in elementary school tend to stop reading for pleasure when they reach middle school and, eventually, stop reading many of their assigned texts.

Children embarking on the personal and social challenges of adolescence stand to gain a great deal from reading widely in texts that are written with them in mind as an audience, texts that present adolescent protagonists coming to grips with personal issues such as developing sexuality, personal goal-setting, friendship, and changes in family relationships, as well as social issues such as racism, environmental damage, censorship, and war. In the classroom, using texts that students perceive as personally relevant will encourage their continued interest in reading as well as introduce them to issues of social justice.

A growing corpus of excellent literature for young adults can meet the need for maintaining interest while introducing social issues. Many novels, short stories, and poems for young adults present a spectrum of protagonists that invite imaginative identification with a range of racial, ethnic, religious, and gender/sexual identities. The young reader from a minority culture finds his or her identity validated when assigned to read a book by an author who shares his or her culture. Gloria Anzaldúa recalls her response to reading, for the first time, a novel by a Chicano: "For days I walked around in stunned amazement that a Chicano could write and could get published. . . . When I saw poetry written in Tex-Mex for the first time, a feeling of pure joy flashed through me. I felt like we really existed as a people" (59-60). In contrast, the young reader from a minority culture who is not assigned books by authors from his or her culture may lose interest. Speaking of his high school English class experience at a point when his previously excellent grades were falling, though he was an avid reader outside the classroom, sociolinguist Keith Gilyard says, "English was on my schedule after gym. When I bothered to stick around, I didn't really participate. I might ask why we couldn't discuss books like *The Outsider* and *Manchild in the Promised Land* only to get a retort in about curriculum and classics" (153). Such texts are equally important for young readers from the majority culture, who gain opportunities to see their world through someone else's eyes.

Yet the great majority of young adult texts that address pressing personal and social issues are not considered when reading lists are prepared for middle school and early high school English classes. There appear to be several reasons for this. First, many YA "problem novels" deal with sensitive subjects, such as nascent sexual activity or alcohol use or the shortcomings of parents. Often, the diction of such texts echoes real people's real conversation, and thus may include language deemed unacceptable in classroom texts. Further, the range of emotional maturity, as well as reading level, shown by students in early adolescence is wide, making it difficult to choose texts on sensitive subjects for whole-class reading and discussion. Another reason that teachers may select canonical texts over YA texts is the increased pressure of standardized texts and standardized curriculum. A review of some state curricular standards, enforced through annual testing, reveals a preference for assigning "classics." A review of recent materials on Advanced Placement courses reveals a strong emphasis on canonical authors, although it is clear that the canon has been expanded to include some minority voices. Efforts to acquaint teachers more fully with multicultural literature, like Arlette Ingram Willis' *Teaching and Using Multicultural Literature in Grades 9-12: Moving Beyond the Canon*, often focus on texts written for adults. What is missing from these lists is any mention of literature for young adults.

Nonetheless, many teachers would be willing to find ways to include such texts, despite the challenges and obstacles to doing so, if they were more familiar with literature for young adults. Gail P. Gregg and Pamela S. Carroll, addressing the reading audience for their *Books and Beyond: Thematic Approaches for Teaching Literature in High School*, write:

> A few years ago, we asked teachers of secondary English to tell us about their classroom practices. The survey results reflected your enthusiasm for teaching literature from and beyond the traditional school canon, but also your frustration—there are so many print and nonprint materials that finding those that are appropriate for your students and implementing them into your curricula is a daunting task. (xi)

Teachers' lack of familiarity is a product of the emphasis on canonical texts they themselves encountered as adolescent readers as well as of the recent proliferation of texts for young adults. We all tend to teach what we know and have ourselves enjoyed, and if what we ourselves know is the canon, because that is what we read in our high school English classes and in many of our college classes, we have compelling reasons to perpetuate the tradition. As Victor Villanueva notes in his autobiographical *Bootstraps: From an American Academic of Color*,

> A manuscript in the mail: "Would you please review this bibliography of Mexican American literature?" He enjoys the literature well enough, Galarza and Anaya and others. But he knows more of Chaucer and Milton and Yeats than of Puerto Rican writers like Piri Thomas or Tato Laviera or Nicolasa Mohr. He knows Mexicans less. (xiii)

Conversations that I have had with English Education majors confirm that the majority of their high school reading has revolved around the canon. Most of these English Education majors are also sophisticated readers, who stopped choosing YA literature for pleasure several years before college, and, even if they remember enjoying some YA texts, they often do not remember specific authors or titles, nor are they familiar with recent YA titles and new authors.

The Young Adult Literature, or YAL, course offers opportunities to introduce pre-service teachers to texts of high literary quality that they may choose for whole-class reading or recommend to individual students, at the same time as it offers opportunities for discussing the rationale for choosing multicultural literature. A YAL course that will give students the confidence to weave YA texts into their classrooms should accomplish three purposes. First, it should promote students' reading widely in texts that present a spectrum of cultures and viewpoints; only if they are acquainted with a variety of texts will they be prepared to make the best possible choices for whole-class reading and small-group assignment or make well-timed and appropriate recommendations for individual readers. Second, the effective YAL course should foster students' ability to assess the literary quality of a text on its own merits rather than on the basis of received opinion, so that they may confidently argue for a new text's inclusion in the classroom or defend its merit if it is challenged. Third, pre-service teachers benefit from learning about pedagogical practices that integrate YAL into standard classroom content and becoming acquainted with resources that will ensure continued development of their knowledge of YAL.

Thus, the course should help them think about *what* texts they may use, *why* they should teach YAL, and *how* they may include YAL in their teaching, so that they may foster their own students' personal growth, empathy, and concern for social justice, at the same time as they foster growth in literacy and critical thinking abilities.

One of the first issues that arises in a YAL class is the difficulty of defining it as a genre. Features typical of many YA novels include length of two hundred pages or less, full character development of only one central character aged thirteen to nineteen, representation of only one character's point of view, presence of no more than one subplot, and fairly fast-paced narrative. Exceptions to this characterization abound, of course, especially with regard to multiple points of view. Alice Childress' *A Hero Ain't Nothin' But a Sandwich* tells the story of thirteen-year-old Benjie's downward spiral into drug use and his increasing alienation from friends, family, and caring teachers through short chapters presenting many characters' points of view. Paul Fleischman's *Seedfolks* similarly tells the story of a multicultural neighborhood's coming together around a community garden through short chapters portraying the points of view of neighbors of varied age and ethnic and racial origin. While these novels create a unified narrative, short story collections like Judith Ortiz Cofer's *An Island Like You: Stories of the Barrio,* can be used as whole texts that collectively present a Latino neighborhood, though each story stands on its own as a whole text. Mel Glenn's popular portrayals of high school lives and drama, like *Who Killed Mr. Chippendale? A Mystery in Poems*, present multiple points of view in short poems that collectively tell a single story. All of these texts are slim volumes that hold high interest for young readers. Texts that violate the length factor as well as the typical focus on a single teen-aged character can hold equal interest, however, as witnessed in the popularity of Ann Brashares' *Sisterhood of the Traveling Pants*, a three hundred page compendium of four friends' interwoven but separate summer stories told by each and only loosely unified by their bond of friendship.

Further experimentation with genre occurs with variation on the popular diary mode that young readers have been widely exposed to through the Dear America series. Virginia Euwer Wolff's *Make Lemonade* evolves through short first-person chapters that are arranged on the page like poetry, telling of fourteen year old LaVaughn's increasing involvement with the family of the seventeen year old single mother for whom she babysits. Margaret Peterson Haddix's *Don't You Dare Read This, Mrs. Dunphrey* takes the form of a journal kept for English class. Rodman Philbrick's *Freak the Mighty* is a narrative by a teenager with a learning disability, followed by an idiosyncratic dictionary of terms by his brilliant terminally ill friend. In Stephen Chbosky's *The Perks of Being a Wallflower*, the protagonist tells the story of his freshman year through a diary-like series of letters to an unspecified recipient. Rob Thomas' *Rats Saw God* intertwines the story of Steve York's senior year in a California high school with Steve's autobiographical "novel" of his junior year living in Texas with his father. Walter Dean Myers' *Monster* alternates a teen inmate's diary with a screenplay he's writing of his trial as it occurs. Another of Paul Fleischman's multivoiced novels, *Seek*, is in the form of a radio show composed by a high school senior in response to a school assignment to write his autobiography.

More significant than the problem of defining genre is the range of issues and problems confronted by characters representing a spectrum of race, ethnicity, sexual orientation, and class. In the above listing, these include drug use, racism, suicide, teen pregnancy, physical abuse, alcoholism, single-parent households, a parent's remarriage, school violence, armed robbery, arrest, heterosexual and same-sex first sexual experiences, sexual harassment on the job, friends' and parents' deaths, depression, learning disabilities, and class differences within a school community. The issues come more than one to a book, opening the door to wide-ranging and meaningful classroom discussions. Despite the serious problems encountered by youthful protagonists, several of the books listed here nevertheless make effective use of humor, an appealing feature that helps to maintain reader interest.

Alleen Pace Nilsen and Kenneth L. Donelson confront the difficulty of simply defining the genre "young adult" in Chapter 1 of their textbook *Literature for Today's Young Adults*, by defining it as "anything that readers between the approximate ages of 12 and 18 choose to read (as opposed to what they may be coerced to read for class assignments)" (3). The difficulty of defining the genre points to some of the difficulties involved in establishing a YA text's value for instruction. The texts listed here lack the canonical status that "classic" texts have; only one of them, *A Hero Ain't Nothin' But a Sandwich*, was written before 1990. One of these authors has warranted a Twayne United States Authors Series volume, but that volume predated the text listed here. *Monster* won several awards, and most—but not all—of these books have been listed as ALA (American Library Association) Best Books for Young Adults. Two of the novels are first novels, a circumstance that virtually guarantees little or no published criticism. So how will a secondary teacher establish the literary merit of YA titles?

Pre-service teachers must reorient their aesthetic values from reliance on published criticism and the "test of time" in determining the literary quality of texts they read. Nilsen and Donelson note that "fewer than two dozen people in the United States are full-time reviewers of juvenile books" (315). Given the paucity of good reviews, pre-service teachers are best prepared to evaluate texts when they think of themselves as practicing literary critics. Becoming an independent critic not only involves mastery of the vocabulary of conventional formalist criticism but also the ability to render a feminist or Marxist critical reading, in order to give a receptive reading to texts that challenge dominant cultural values. In her argument for teaching theory, *Critical Encounters in High School English: Teaching Literary Theory to Adolescents*, Deborah Appleman underscores the relevance of feminist and Marxist theory when she mentions these similarities: ". . . they both are political, they both interrogate textual features with considerations of power and oppression, they both invite us to consider the kinds of prevailing ideologies that help construct the social realities in which we participate (or sometimes become unwitting participants)" (58). As well as becoming confident judges of texts on their own merits, pre-service teachers will find it useful to learn about the professional organizations and journals that give awards for new YA books, publish lists of "best" books, and review young adult literature.

Above all, the students in a YAL class should become comfortable with the idea of endorsing books that may not reinforce standards of excellence that they have come to expect in canonical works. The diction of YA texts, for example, is colloquial, slangy, and "ungrammatical" by school standards. The narrator of Walter Dean Myers' *Hoops* introduces a character like this:

> The cat is laying there singing some kind of weird song. . . . I reached down and grabbed him by the collar and started to drag him off the court, and then, all of a sudden, he' up. Not only is he up, but he's got this blade in my face! I dropped the ball and backed off. This guy smells like somebody done peed in bad wine and washed his teeth in it, but he's got this knife, and he's bigger than me. (8)

And the narrator of Chris Crutcher's *The Crazy Horse Electric Game* describes an encounter like this:

> Willie is absolutely fixed on Lacey's son. He knows only the skeleton of the story behind all this, but, from his core, knows instantly this is *family* gone crazy. It comes in a flash: the boy before him is wrecked; the man beneath his feet, desperately holding on with everything he's got to stay just above the quicksand. This is what happens when we astonish ourselves with our capacity to be vicious; when we realize so late how our expectations have betrayed us. (150)

Some readers are worried that these deviations from standards taught in school writing and grammar classes may have a negative impact on adolescents' literacy development. Their practice of criticism that validates such diction will help them become more comfortable with a range of varieties of English, as well as with the viewpoints that are expressed in these varieties. Pre-service teachers' conviction of the quality of such texts will prepare them for curricular challenges.

Equally important in preparing for possible curricular challenges is acquaintance with resources for fighting censorship, such as the American Library Association's *Newsletter on Intellectual Freedom, Intellectual Freedom Manual,* and *Hit List: Frequently Challenged Books for Young Adults* and the CD *Rationales for Challenged Books* prepared by the National Council of Teachers of English with the International Reading Association.

And finally, pre-service teachers who have a repertoire of sound pedagogical practices for incorporating Young Adult Literature in their classrooms, along with a conviction of its value, will be most successful in presenting multicultural literature in their classrooms. Publications on pedagogy abound, including National Council of Teachers of English journals such as *English Journal* and *The ALAN Review* (the publication of the Assembly on Literature for Adolescents of NCTE). These publications often include up-to-date annotated lists of multicultural literature. Books such as Joan F. Kaywell's four volumes on *Adolescent Literature as a Complement to the Classics* present classroom practices for bridging the gap between students' reading interest with mandated curricular reading. Gail P. Gregg and Pamela S. Carroll's

Books and Beyond: Thematic Approaches for Teaching Literature in High School suggest ways to integrate non-print and popular materials into more traditional literature and social studies instruction. Lois Thomas Stover's *Young Adult Literature: The Heart of the Middle School Curriculum* suggests cross-disciplinary links for team-teaching projects. Pre-service teachers should be assigned writing and research projects that encourage them to think about how they may use YA texts in their own classrooms as well as to think critically about the literary value of these texts. Furthermore, these students should be encouraged to make their own contributions to the critical and pedagogical literature on YA texts.

When he surveyed college instructors of Young Adult Literature courses in 1999, David Gill discovered:

> Professors teaching adolescent literature courses do indeed value multicultural literature, both in theory and in practice. Unlike other surveys of comparative groups, I found little evidence that only books written by white males formed the core of readings assigned in young adult literature courses. The respondents in this study, to use a hackneyed phrase, do seem to preach what they practice and practice what they preach.

Reading and studying young adult literature provides many opportunities for discussing social justice. Preparing pre-service teachers to continue these discussions in their own classrooms requires that we not only introduce multicultural texts of high literary value but also, perhaps to a greater extent than in any other literature course, encourage students to become independent literary critics and full partners in the professional community of teacher-scholars.

Works Cited

Anzaldúa, Gloria. *Borderlands/La Frontera: The New Mestiza*. San Francisco: Aunt Lute Books, 1987.

Applebee, Arthur N. *Tradition and Reform in the Teaching of English: A History*. Urbana, IL: National Council of Teachers of English, 1974.

Appleman, Deborah. *Critical Encounters in High School English: Teaching Literary Theory to Adolescents*. New York: Teachers College Press and National Council of Teachers of English, 2000.

Brashares, Ann. *Sisterhood of the Traveling Pants*. New York: Delacorte, 2001.

Chbosky, Stephen. *The Perks of Being a Wallflower*. New York: Pocket Books, 1999.

Childress, Alice. *A Hero Ain't Nothin' But a Sandwich*. 1973; rpt. New York: Puffin, 2000.

Crutcher, Chris. *The Crazy Horse Electric Game*. New York: Greenwillow, 1987.

Fleischman, Paul. *Seedfolks*. 1997. New York: HarperTrophy, 1999.

Gill, David. "A National Survey of the Use of Multicultural Young Adult Literature in University Courses." *The ALAN Review* 27.2 (2000). 6 May 2002. <http://scholar.lib.vt.edu/ejournals/ALAN/winter00/gill.html>.

Gilyard, Keith. *Voices of the Self: A Study of Language Competence*. Detroit: Wayne State University Press, 1991.

Glenn, Mel. *Who Killed Mr. Chippendale? A Mystery in Poems*. 1996. New York: Puffin, 1999.

Gregg, Gail P., and Pamela S. Carroll, eds. *Books and Beyond: Thematic Approaches for Teaching Literature in High School*. Norwood, MA: Christopher-Gordon, 1998.

Haddix, Margaret Peterson. *Don't You Dare Read This, Mrs. Dunphrey*. New York: Simon & Schuster, 1996.

Kaywell, Joan F. *Adolescent Literature as a Complement to the Classics*. Vols. 1-4. Norwood, MA: Christopher-Gordon, 1993-2000.

Myers, Walter Dean. *Hoops*. 1983. New York: Laurel Leaf, 1999.

----------. *Monster*. New York: HarperCollins, 1999.

National Council of Teachers of English with the International Reading Association. *Rationales for Challenged Books.* CD-ROM. Urbana, IL: National Council of Teachers of English, 1998.

Nilsen, Alleen Pace, and Kenneth L. Donelson. *Literature for Today's Young Adults.* 6th ed. New York: Longman, 2001.

Office for Intellectual Freedom. *Intellectual Freedom Manual.* 6th ed. Chicago: American Library Association, 2002.

Office for Intellectual Freedom Committee of the Young Adult Library Services Association. *Hit List: Frequently Challenged Books for Young Adults.* Chicago: American Library Association, 1996.

Ortiz Cofer, Judith. *An Island Like You: Stories of the Barrio.* 1995. New York: Puffin, 1996.

Philbrick, Rodman. *Freak the Mighty.* New York: Scholastic, 1993.

Stover, Lois Thomas. *Young Adult Literature: The Heart of the Middle School Curriculum.* Portsmouth, NH: Heinemann-Boynton/Cook, 1996.

Thomas, Rob. *Rats Saw God.* New York: Simon & Schuster, 1996.

Villanueva, Victor. *Bootstraps: From an American Academic of Color*. Urbana, IL: National Council of Teachers of English, 1993.

Willis, Arlette Ingram, ed. *Teaching and Using Multicultural Literature in Grades 9-12: Moving beyond the Canon*. Norwood, MA: Christopher-Gordon Publishers, 1998.

Wolff, Virginia Euwer. *Make Lemonade*. 1993. New York: Point, 1994.

Nightjohn: "'Cause to know things, for us to know things, is bad for them. We get to wanting and when we get to wanting it's bad for them. They thinks we want what they got . . . That's why they don't want us reading."

Sarny: " ... I didn't know what letters was, nor what they meant, but I thought it might be something I wanted to know. To learn."

Sarny: "Late he come walking and nobody else knows, nobody from the big house or the other big houses, know but we do. We know. Late he come walking and it be Nightjohn and he bringing us the way to know."

from *Nightjohn*

Gary Paulsen

Reflections on Language, Gender, Class, and Power Relations with Suggestions for Instructional Applications

Ines Senna Shaw

My purpose in this article is twofold: to share some of my reflections and ideas distilled from various disciplines about gender, class, race and ethnicity, power relations, and language, and to offer suggestions for instructional applications that provide a framework for students to think critically about how the complex aspects of our lives in society are connected. The division of intellectual approaches into disciplinary units and courses, from grade school (e.g., language arts, social studies, science) to college (e.g., English, sociology, biology), and the tendency for teacher-scholars to work within these disciplines contribute to the compartmentalization of not only what is studied but also the isolation of student bodies. For example, students may explore notions of femininity and masculinity through textual analysis in language arts or the English classroom, but will they learn to make connections between these notions and welfare policies, crime levels, their mothers' salary, or the way they live in the same classroom or during the same term? Intellectual work needs to be less wed to disciplinary conceptual frameworks and practices. An interdisciplinary approach helps pull together knowledge, perspectives, and methodologies not normally available within different fields of study so that students can understand the complex interplay of differences and social relations. The democratic principles and the practices that critical pedagogies embody need to be modeled in the classroom.

Both scholarship and the desire to transform the classroom are being driven by the need to see oneself in representations of reality. Adrienne Rich captures the dissonance one feels at not seeing oneself in represented realities: there is "a moment of psychic disequilibrium, as if you looked into a mirror and saw nothing" (199). Scholarly interest in how language, as an integrated component of human experience, mediates thought and represents and shapes reality sharply rose during and after the civil rights and women's rights movements in mid-twentieth-century. Simultaneously, awareness of how language reflects racial and gender biases was popularized and paralleled by the social changes engendered by these movements. Class, dis/ability, and sexual orientation concerns in the following decades continued to fan scholarly interest in how language affects individuals and social groups, and how language itself is affected by power relations and social changes. Clearly a great deal of progress has been made in these areas. However, schools need to work more to help pre-teen and teenage students to connect more as members of society, and in this process, come to understand how personal relations shape society, and in turn, how society shapes these relations. In other words, for social justice to be more than an abstract concept, an understanding of the mutuality of this process and of the interconnectedness of our lives is essential.

Since the 1960s, studies have been conducted on gendered differences in language use; stylistic characteristics of women's language and writing; the use of prestigious and non-prestigious variants and their correlations to sex, class, ethnicity, age, social networks, and speech events; the relationship of words and syntax to gender in a variety of genres and rhetorical and social contexts; and the ways in which power relations are manifested in and through language in social interactions, both in written and oral forms (or conversation). Explanations, analyses, and interpretations have been offered from several theoretical perspectives (some of which have centered around the sex-specific socialization experiences outside the context of power relations). All levels of education were thus inevitably affected by such interests and the knowledge produced by them, the impetus of social transformations gradually extending into pedagogy. Several generations have now profited from instructional applications of this vast sociocultural knowledge production, and it is not unusual for high school students entering college to have some degree of awareness of racially- and gender-biased behaviors, and to a lesser extent, of how language demeans or stereotypes people in terms of dis/ability, and sexual orientation.

A great deal of the work related to gender in the 6-12 grades has focused on language use, and particularly on talk; gender (in)equity in sports and reading materials; gender inequality and sexist practices in the classroom and education in general (for example, how female and male students are treated, talk, or talked to differently, and write); gender in literature (for example, representations and images of women); and, to a lesser extent, gender equity and sexist language in assessment and career counseling (and in respect to the latter, this has been particularly relevant to math and science). The relations between language and gender have typically been equated with sexist language use and practices, and sometimes expressed in a discourse of blame and limited to reductionist, decontextualized, and normative views and attitudes. Moreover, there has been criticism of some aspects of the educational work on sexism and language; for example, some have seen the avoidance of texts that are blatantly sexist as censoring (see Joan Swann 1992: 232, Gemma Moss 1989).

The concern with gender inequalities in the classroom and education seems to have made more headway in the curriculum reform in the British Isles, which has given prominence to several of the aforementioned facets of gender and language. However, as Joan Swann points out, although "'equal opportunities' reminders" can be found in curriculum documents,

> these scattered references have an ambiguous status. Their presence signals official recognition that gender differences and inequalities exist in education and that language plays a part in them; but there is little discussion of these differences and inequalities and virtually no concrete guidance on how to deal with them. (1)

Swann's remark underscores the problem of regarding gender and other social categories as add-ons to the curriculum.

Furthermore, the study of language is no longer limited to the traditional study of grammar. In many classrooms, students take the role of explorers of language and creators of knowledge. In *Gender Issues in the Teaching of English*, Lisa McClure makes valuable suggestions to change the traditional study of language, building on the wealth of studies from linguistics and feminist studies. Attention is given to both spoken and written language. For example, she suggests the collection and analysis of language samples from the speech of a variety of people "in their school and community" and from the students' reading materials so that the students learn to recognize and reflect about "stereotypes and biases in language use." Such a type of study lays the groundwork for the study of sexist language and how stereotyping occurs through language, as the same methods can be employed (39-47). Martino and Mellor's *Gendered Fictions* (2000) focuses a great deal on the exploration of naming and labeling through words and expressions in the search for meanings that reveal different versions of reality. The activities are certain to develop an awareness of gender issues and reading from gendered positions, a competence that aids students as critical thinkers.

Progressive and traditional educators have in common their interest in fostering critical thinking. Two basic differences between them are the beliefs that (i) one of the educator's responsibility is to make explicit the relations of power that guide our behavior and the social inequalities that lead us to think of and treat others in particular ways; and (ii) that disruption of the status quo (e.g., readings, words, and discursive patterns) is necessary in order to produce resistant behavior and achieve an understanding of power politics and its effects on human psyche, behavior, and institution or organization. In Willinsky's view, "the point of a progressive education" is to be equally informed by the goals of reason and democracy" (74). For elementary school teacher Jennifer O'Brien, critical literacy "is an important part of showing children a way of looking at the world so that they don't simply accept things as they are presented to them" (Comber and Nixon 137). The effects of school literacy practices (including progressive practices) must be attended as well because, as Comber and Nixon and other scholars have found, they may unintendendly "maintain disadvantages, may be normative rather than transformative, domesticating rather than liberating, alienating rather connecting," thus failing to democratize the classroom (180).

Moreover, Willinsky believes teachers should be students of their own education (74), and Comber and Nixon remark that "teachers' own life worlds and values mediate the uptake and enactment of pedagogical practices and curriculum theories" (122). Ramalho, a college professor of teacher education, argues that situating our pedagogical practices in our background and life history is important because as educators, we need to know, in an experiential sense, our own pedagogy. Thus, we ask our students to relate what they are learning to personal experience; we teach them to think in terms of relations and to engage in readings and/or analyses of such relations; and we do so with the expectation that such readings and/or analyses will foster a deeper understanding of the subjects under study, whether they are social or scientific facts and issues. From her own pedagogy, informed by her background and life history, concerns for social justice, and feminist and educational theories, there emerges a historically-situated fundamental question that encompasses the individual, the group, and the environment—what does it mean to be a human being on planet Earth today?

While reflecting on what critical thinking and progressive education may mean to students, I was reminded of a question a young student asked me, apparently quite seriously, years ago during a class: "Can't a critical thinker become paranoid?" We were reading Steven Pinker's *The Language Instinct*, and in response, I referred to a joke recounted in the book about "two psychoanalysts who meet on the street. One says, "Good morning;" the other thinks, "I wonder what he meant by that" (230). This teachable moment opened up the door to a discussion of discursive practices and the pragmatics of conversation. My recollection of this event and joke now leads me to think that the issue is not only the detection and measurement of effects, but also of how long they may last, and how they integrate with other influences on our students. These are too large questions for this article, but an example might suffice to illustrate the difficulty of learning whether pedagogy and content effectively meet teachers' goals for the education of their students.

Joan Swann reviews and critiques studies and practices arising from concerns about gender imbalances and inequalities in *Girls, Boys and Language*, including a critique of teachers' responses to students' "stereotyped writing choices" (155). She reaches the conclusion that "gender inequalities do not operate in a straightforward way," (159) and that, although there is "some evidence that books read by children may have an immediate and specific effect on their behavior and expressed attitudes, in the long term, the picture is more complex" (161-62). Notwithstanding the myriad of different portrayals and ideas to which one is exposed, and the fact that the multiplicity of influences make it difficult to sort out conceptual categories singly, the forces that maintain the status quo and the sheer amount of daily exposure to gender, class, racial, dis/ability, and sexual orientation biases and representations, reinforced by gendered behaviors and discursive practices, make the potential long-term, if not lasting, effects of such representations and habituated behaviors and linguistic usages on one's worldview almost certain. Jean Kilbourne, in the series of instructional videos of her lectures, started with *Killing Us Softly*, offers a similar argument in regard to images and their influence on the way identities and representations of reality are formed.

Language is one of the most vital means by which critical thinking skills are developed—as Pinker points out, "language is so tightly woven into human experience that it is scarcely possible to imagine life without it. Chances are that if you find two or more people together anywhere on earth, they will soon be exchanging words" (17). The development of an understanding of the symbolic nature of language and its implications entails knowing that meanings are conventionally created, that words have a history and incorporate the thinking and customs of the people who use it, that words are used and mean different things in specific social contexts, that they reflect and determine one's political perspective, and that they have a psychological dimension (for example, they trigger or induce emotional responses). The traditional study of language at all levels of education emphasized meaning (the dictionary meaning or the denotation) in isolation, but modern pedagogy expanded it to include context, and, consequently, the use and social implications of denotations and connotations. Nevertheless, this study remains localized for the contexts represented in the text under study, and, not infrequently, personal connections in classroom discussions and writing assignments (essays, journal entries) result in students drawing generalizations based on narrow personal experiences. Extending the parameters of the bridges teachers attempt to establish between the personal and the external world may help students extend their world of reference.

Particular attention also needs to be paid to language ideology and the manner in which they are reproduced in discursive practices. The ideology of superiority of man over woman is entrenched in our discursive practices and is thus in a cycle of continuous reinforcement through its daily reproduction in language use in the multitude of social interactions that take place everyday. One of the main elements of this regular practice is the definition of males in terms of attributes of general humanity making it possible for words representing the attribute of being male to be non-gendered, "general representatives of human or all people," and the gender-specific definition of girls and women in terms of culturally-defined and assigned attributes for femaleness and femininity, making them gendered individuals (Black and Coward 114-17). As is widely known by now by those familiar with feminism, the 1850 Act of British Parliament that codified this universal representation by declaring that nouns and pronouns referring to females, such as *woman* and *she*, were to be understood to be implied by nouns and pronouns referring to males, such as *man* and *he*. Most instructional activity centers on sexism that affects girls and women. While this focus is necessary since girls and women are the ones most widely affected by sexism, we must work *concurrently* to help students not only become aware of what the non-gendering of males and the gendering of females entail, but also analyze this phenomenon, starting in the classroom.

Ideologies work to establish and maintain the status quo. They justify all sorts of unequal opportunities and unfair policies of access to and distributions of resources, burdens, rewards, prestige, and wealth. Language ideologies control people's voices, both in classrooms and society at large, making bodies invisible or not count in a political sense. In Thompson's words, Bourdieu notes that "individuals speak with different degrees of authority" and "words are loaded with unequal weights, depending on who utters them and how they are said" (1). Clearly, students, as well as teachers, can benefit from an understanding of how power relations affect language in the classroom. Researchers, such as Peirce (1995) and McKay and Wong (1996), have pointed out, for example, that power relations between speakers may contribute to the degree to which ESL students are able or not to communicate. Students who come from speech communities and who speak nonstandard dialects also speak with less authority than those whose speech includes standard features of vocabulary and pronunciation; furthermore, their speech condemns them to a more or less desperate attempt to be correct—or to silence (97). In socially-stratified societies and countries, such as the United States and other countries in the Americas with significant populations of immigrants, classifying languages and dialects as bad, proper, or good works as a smokescreen for class and racial issues.

In Linda Christensen's view, it is vitally important to help students become aware that power relations inform our classifications of language as standard and nonstandard:

> If I do not teach students that the standard language is not based on the 'best' language but on the language that the powerful, the ruling class, developed, then every time I "correct" their home language, I am condemning it as wrong, as incorrect, as "nonstandard." If I fail to make that social blueprint transparent, I endorse it. (54-55)

The real significance of Ebonics is the implication of the students' speech variety and way of speaking (dialect or language, depending on one's linguistic and political perspectives) to their life; in this sense, the situation is the same for countless of children entering and in schools throughout the U.S. who speak dialects different from the desirable standard. Ebonics was the star or the villain, depending on one's perspective, that brought socially-related linguistic differences to the surface, but hardly a splash was made by the class and racial issues connected with it, the machinery of the status quo making it seem as if this was merely the educational matter of teaching the students the forms of the language necessary for them to get a job!

Paul Gee calls the contextualized patterns of experiences and associations related to linguistic meanings "situated meanings," that is, "correlations of various features" (46). They are "a product of the bottom-up action and reflection with which the learner engages the world and of the top-down guidance of the cultural models (theories) the learner is developing or being apprenticed to" (47). Thus, "one's body and mind have to be able to be situated with—coordinated by and with—these correlated features in the world" (46). The body in its physical and material forms matters because as such, it is always described in terms of relations characterized by [cultural] values and [social] judgments (Costa 40-41). One of the social dimensions of the body is accrued from the way it is spoken of, seen or looked, and is a site of contested difference. Color as a metaphor of the body allows for an investigative reading of this dimension. In addition to movement and appearance, color comes to embody both socio-historical site and identity.

Rosa reports on an activity that she observed in a Brazilian grade school classroom. The teacher, suspecting that tensions among students arose from a dimension of the body, devised a lesson to look at the body from the lens of ethnicity. Students engaged in a series of activities: writing, drawing, cutting out pictures, playful games, and problem-solving cases. An analysis of the productions of the children revealed that color is associated with aesthetic and religious values, demonstration of affection, erotic games, male oppression, and scents, such as the odor of sweat, specifically articulated as the "smell of blacks" or 'cheiro de nego' (42). According to Iris Young, race (race/color in the Brazilian context) of socially non-dominant groups is stereotyped and marked out by members of socially dominant groups, who, in turn, "occupy an unmarked, neutral, apparently universal position"—their visibility need not be commented upon (129). From feminist theories, some of which are informed by Foucault's theory of "docile bodies" and some by diverse female experiences and material histories, we understand that the female body is a site of violence.[1] The body is indeed a matter of great importance for teaching and learning.

The word "body" elicits personal connections, often associated to being thin or fat, or just right, and reaches deeper in the psyche where memories of present and past situations reside. These situations create an awareness, not always made conscious at surface level or externalized, of one's position relative to others in hierarchies of power. We feel, as the littlest children with some level of awareness of the self, the transgressions of space when our bodies are touched, whether during a bath as a parent, perhaps lovingly, scrubs an arm or the back; the smarting pain of a smack on the butt or the face; the pressure of fingers as we are lifted to be held by an adult standing up. The mind selects some memories, sometimes apparently inconsequential, sometimes deeply hurtful, and brings them up, again at various levels of consciousness when we see or experience situations in which someone else's body is affected. A picture in a magazine of a woman holding a child of about five or six years of age reminds a student of an uncle who used to pick her up and then go round and round with her. He would let go of his hands on her back and her upper body would move backwards while she sat on his arms and he would hold her legs. She recalled the pleasure she felt as they swirled (she would stretch her arms and loved the swift current of air under her flying hair) and the pain of the pressure of his fingers digging into her skin. Pain and pleasure—real phenomena that student bodies experience everyday throughout their lives.

As a site of enactment of power relations and of an experiential dimension of identity formation, the body doesn't exist apart from its relation to society and its members. The black body has been both subject and object of violence, which, according to Cornell West, has been fueled by a white supremacist ideology that instills fear and contempt both inwardly and outwardly (85). The education of children cannot consider only the label "children" because the body of real students is formed from historical and current conditions that affect their psyche and material form. My own memory of a situation involving the conflation of these dimensions of the body is imprinted in a particular time and location and was awakened by a conversation with a colleague in the process of preparing for a conference presentation. He was telling me about a reading that described a Native American cultural practice of punishment by having a person kneel over grains of corn. Instantaneously there was a little "I," kneeling on grains of corn in the cement backyard of my grandparents' home in a small town in rural Brazil. Next to me was a young servant some six to eight years older than I who also knelt over grains of corn, while my grandmother's shrill voice (or as I would say in Brazilian Portuguese, in a *voz esganiçada*) instructed us not to slouch and to keep our arms stretched open as well. The corn uncomfortably and painfully dug into our skin, as readers can imagine.

What is significant, however, is the hierarchy of power relations enacted in this situation. Aside from the display of power of my grandmother over us, her position as older person (age), grandmother (familial relationship), and boss (employer-employee relations), our nonexternalized consciousness of class privilege differences and our positions in these hierarchies of power enabled me to know that I could engage in transgression by lowering my arms when my grandmother walked away and get up when "I" felt I had paid enough of a penalty for whatever infraction of behavior we had committed without any real consequence (because of my awareness that my parents stood at a higher rung of authority) and enabled this young maid to know that she could not without risking her physical and material well-being (her employment was her means of support, and possibly a contribution to the support of her family).

The social dimensions of language in relation to the body can and should be studied from K-12 and in college because, like language, the body is a fundamental aspect of the question of who we are as human beings, and because it touches every aspect of our lives. An understanding of how bodies are constructed and issues involving their integrity can begin with explorations of different patterns of experiences. Teachers can bring store-bought greeting cards, including birth announcements; students can examine advertisements of dolls and toys for girls and boys and observe and describe how students and community members are dressed in a variety of contexts, paying attention to types, texture, and design of clothes and colors.[2] Hues of color, such as pastel green, or deep green are important because they are associated with males/masculinity and females/femininity. Lessons in classification along a sex and gender, female/femininity and male/masculinity continuum can be developed. The variations that come about in the biological development of humans into female and male can also be mapped into a continuum and juxtaposed onto the other continuum. The previous observations, descriptions, and examinations of how people dress and how the media represent them can then be compared. This comparison may be extended to the fashion industry's selection of very young models of certain genetic types, the relation of this and other industries' deceptive strategies to the social constructions of femaleness/femininity and maleness/masculinity, and how the body is affected by such constructions. The political dimension of these connections should be explored alongside the economic dimension, so that students are able to relate looks, bodies, social constructions, class interest, profit, and harm.

Bodies are sexualized by virtue of the readings that they are exposed to from birth to death (Santos 106).[3] The body may be an instrument of realization of sexual desire, although sexual acts and the body are e popularly interchangeably and confusedly named for sexual orientation preference (e.g., lesbian, queer). There is a growing body of scholarship on language and sexuality that explores the social and political dimensions of sexual identity, linguistic practices, and language ideologies in different cultural settings and from multiple perspectives.[4] Teachers can help high school students explore language and various facets of the sexuality dimension of the body, including societal issues of oppression of the most vulnerable in hierarchies of power. For example, the embodiment in language of body types and the associated vocabulary of dieting and body-related illnesses; the moral dimension of sexuality as reflected in normative language; language representing the stratification of the body in class relations; poetic language and the body; the language of beauty, body language, and sexuality as commodities.

Because single words or expressions are used to characterize different events and associations, they can serve as the starting point for associations that cross disciplinary boundaries. As Gee explains, "a word such as *coffee*, for instance, appears to be a 'general term,' standing for a general, decontextualized concept. But . . . *coffee* is associated with a number of more specific patterns of experience tied to particular contexts" (44). Using Vygotsky's theory of learning, Gee elaborates that teachers can help a child to use "concepts in a reflective, controlled, and conscious way" by helping the child focus on "consciously on conceptual connections, verbal links, and connections between form and meaning" (49-50). A concept is partially understood by virtue of its connections to other concepts, such as causation, responsibility, and contingency, among others (50).

Students at all levels should learn to explore the implications and effects of labeling, naming, and name (re-)appropriating, particularly in regard to gender, race or ethnicity, sexual orientation, and sexual identity. Naming and names are "a culture's way of fixing what will *count* as reality in a universe of overwhelming, chaotic sensations, development of a multitude of possible realities" (Cameron 9). Such explorations will help them develop a greater awareness of conflicts engendered by the theoretical model of sex and gender that organizes humans into distinct categories of females and males. They will also sharpen their ability to see connections between attitudes, behaviors, and language. Naming and labels dictate patterns of behavior toward those to whom the labels and names are applied and are most powerful when driven by ideologies. Take the ideology that certain people—those who are labeled in terms of a color other than "white" and do not appear to have much money—are inferior intellectually and less capable, incapable, or unreliable than those who are not "colored" and have money because of inherent flaws of different sorts. This ideology is realized in common discursive practices that name disparate behaviors and states of affairs, from the child who doesn't bring her homework to school, to the toys scattered in the yard or a cracked car window: "they create their own poverty;" "you know how these people are . . .;" "the problem is that they don't like to work."

As Allport points out, the saliency of the feature that is picked out for a label may prevent alternative conceptualizations and classifications (248). People are predisposed or led to behave differently according to the salient feature and ideologically driven pre-assumptions and associations. The man labeled "spic" is not treated the same way as the man labeled "Chicano" is, who is not treated the same way a man labeled "Mexican-American" is, who is not treated the same way as a man labeled "British" is. The labels "right" and "left" also provide a good illustration of this phenomenon. A person in the right-mind (sane, logical, sensible) does not dispense left-handed (unjust, illogical, unreasonable) compliments. The left-handed are "different;" "awkward;" "mixed-up;" "socially gauche;" "not the norm" or "difficult," and require special accommodations. The right-handed are "dexterous;" "adroit;" the norm. The social consequences of labels are immense—they affect laws, policies, regulations, attitudes, personal and professional relationships.

As stated earlier, words or expressions can serve as starting points for an understanding of the "larger and specific sociocultural coordinations of which they are a part and in which they gain their significance" (Gee 52). The political and economic dimensions of social issues should to be considered in the language arts and English class in order for students to expand their world of reference and learn to integrate their personal experience into the larger context of the experiences of others unlike and like them. Below are questions and issues that teachers may use to guide students' discussions and assignments; implied in these questions is the idea that power is negotiated in different contexts, and that the oppressed also exercise agency:

Political dimension: Who makes the decisions, and for whom? With whom does the authority reside? How is that authority assigned? How is that authority employed? Who recognizes this authority? Who must abide by decisions? Do they have a choice, and if so, what does it entail? If they want to abide by the decisions, are there alternative courses of action, and if so, what are they? Who benefits from the decisions, policies, rules, regulations, or laws? Who stands on the margins? Who speaks in public? Who may speak in public? (different questions!) What effect do the voices that are heard publicly have? What are the consequences for the silenced voices? How can they be heard? What ideologies are embedded in political discursive practices? Whose interests do they represent? How do they privilege some and disadvantage others?

Economic: Who owns the resources? Who owns property and land? Who has access to resources and property? What enables the access to resources and property? What prevents it? Who does not own property and land? Why not? How are the resources distributed? Who distributes them? Who receives them? What conditions exist for particular patterns of distribution? Who does not get a piece of the pie, and why not? Where are the resources and wealth accumulated? Why? Who works in what? Who has access to what jobs, and why? How can conditions change? What ideologies are embedded in the economic discursive practices? Whose interests do they represent? How do they privilege some and disadvantage others? Will changes in distribution and access bring about benefits? Do these changes represent mere redistribution of and access to resources and wealth, or do they result in changes in ideologies and the structure of society?

Work: The connections that this word engenders can teach students that the objective reality (the things we do) is apprehended differently, and that these differences result partly from the ways we organize social life and partly from our naming them. Both influence and shape our discursive practices and personal relations to others in social interactions, our relations to institutions and organizations, and how we are perceived and treated by others. Students can collect data to the question "do you work?" The responses should come from women and men in a variety of contexts but should definitely include stay-at-home women, possibly from the U.S. and from other countries for cultural variations to emerge. Students can also journal about their own activities, whether they think of them as work, and, if they can, reflect on why. I don't think that there is a necessary developmental sequence here, even though our typical methodologies of composition, for example, call for personal explorations first. It is too simple to say that work means salaried work. Women who work at home many times are paid in money for their services; for example, some women get "an allowance" to buy not only groceries but clothes and other things for themselves. Practically, they are getting this money for the service they render, even though it is hard for most people to think this way because language does not call this payment "salary" but "allowance." The number of connections that this word can trigger is limitless, and the boundaries that teachers may have to set have to do with their knowledge of subjects (although they should allow more for students' agency and not retain for themselves the major responsibility for knowledge production); educational outcomes; and time.

Sweat: This at first may appear to be a strange word, but it intimately connected with work. Teachers can start by asking questions, such as, "Who sweats more, a secretary or CEO?" "A farmer or a symphony conductor?" "A housewife or a janitor?" "Who sweats more in your house?" These questions can help students start thinking about class issues and distribution of resources and wealth. In the place of work, CEOs' offices are typically in higher floors, may have windows that open, have air-conditioned offices, space, comfort, and quiet. Age and disability intersect with class—when big cities go through a heat wave, among the first casualties are the old, the retired, the old women, the disable on fixed, low income, who live in the lower floors, who must keep their windows closed because of crime in the neighborhood, and who sometimes do not even own a fan. Teachers who want to add a historical dimension to the connections to **work** and **sweat** (shops) can show a documentary segment of the Triangle Shirtwaist Company tragedy in the CNN-produced video "Centuries of Women." Students can become aware of both the improvements in workers' conditions over the last century, of the situations that reproduce the same or similar conditions of old in factories nowadays, and of the social actions undertaken by activists that work toward fairness of treatment and conditions for such workers.

Master: Students can learn that words have a historical dimension, that denotations change as a result of changes in connotations, and that we do not all share the same knowledge of the social, emotional, and historical dimensions of words. As feminists have pointed out, the power relations captured in the discursive uses of terms master and mistress are quite different, and activities can be provided for students to explore such uses in the popular media (for example, in detective stories, cartoons, comic books, or movies). In addition to exploring the meanings of master across time in terms of its gender and class implications, students can draw connections to science through its language. A dominant genetic theory of DNA postulates the existence of a **master** molecule that controls gene action. Thus, a parallel can be drawn between this hierarchical organization and social hierarchies (for example, father as head of the family; the Catholic priest, the father of his flock; the rabbi, the head of his congregation; the farm owner as the master of slaves; the president of the university as the master of the academic organization). Students can explore whether the social hierarchy in their school breaks or conforms to such patterns. A lesson in cause and effect can also be drawn from this connection. Students can learn that a scientist's lack of awareness or failure to see the cultural lens from which she or he examines a phenomenon may prevent this scientist from considering a different but valid scientific explanation. Teachers can assign portions of two of Barbara McClintock's biographies as an illustration of this lesson, and to problematize the issue of reputation. McClintock is a cytogeneticist who is most known for her discovery of transposable elements in maize in 1946, and for receiving the Nobel Prize in 1983. (The two recommended biographies are Nathaniel C. Comfort's "Two genes, no enzyme: a second look at Barbara McClintock and the 1951 Cold Spring Harbor Symposium" and Evelyn Fox Keller's *A Feeling for the Organism*).

Making connections does not mean that teachers will not do what they traditionally do. For example, the use of first-person accounts, the students' or other authors', create opportunities for the practical teaching of grammar and punctuation (reported in direct speech, for example) and literature. Below is a poem by a Yiddish poet that teachers can use as a model for a writing assignment. They can ask students to write a poem describing their own activities and the conditions under which they perform them. Students can also be encouraged to bring lyrics and other writings that explore the connections they are making to work, for example. The following poem not only describes the conditions of a sweatshop but reproduces the repetitiveness of the work both rhetorically and linguistically:

> I work, and I work, without rhyme, without reason—
> Produce and produce, and produce without end.
> For what? And for whom? I don't know, I don't wonder—since when can a whirling machine comprehend?
> No feelings, no thoughts, not the least understanding;
>> This bitter, this murderous drudgery drains
>> The noblest, the finest, the best and the richest,
>> The deepest, the highest that living contains.
> Away rush the seconds, the minutes and the hours;
> Each day and each night like a wind-driven sail;
> I drive the machine, as though eager to catch them,
> I drive without reason—no hope, no avail.

The importance of re-naming experiences in the classroom cannot be overstated. As Van Den Bergh asserts,

> changing language raises consciousness. It brings to public attention the deceptions inherent within words to dispel them. Through such an exorcism, renaming makes public a political statement, and it empowers the group by giving it a sense of control over life. Renaming is the politics of personal experience. Therefore, the way in which one names one's experience has profound implications extending beyond the individual (134).

I would add that re-naming experiences not only bring deceptions to light but also expand our world of reference.

Thus, re-naming the experience of language enlarges the conceptualization of it as merely a field of study to the ubiquitous embodiment of experience.

It is not uncommon after a discussion in which alternative perspectives and views are aired for a teacher to end it with a statement of consensus. However, as Bruffee has convincingly argued, consensus not infrequently amounts to one view or perspective of the world, which then in the context of the classroom community, becomes dominant and silences or prevents others from being considered or valued. Consensus, however, is not a defining criterion of community, although it may be desirable on specific occasions. The suggested applications do not call consensus building—they are meant to be open-ended and allow students to continue drawing connections even after a particular class session.

In conclusion, we want our students to discover their potential, grow intellectually, develop skills, transfer what they learn to new situations, make needed adaptations, know how to communicate appropriately in writing and orally, and maintain attitudes and values that will help them have productive and successful personal and professional lives. As socially and politically conscious educators concerned with justice, we also want to train our students to be critical thinkers not only in the traditional sense of thinking logically and tuning their argumentative skills, but also in the modern sense of being able to understand the socio-cultural dimensions of language and life in society. At the same time, we must be cognizant that "critical literacy is not formulaic, " that it cannot "be characterized as a single approach or method of teaching"(Comber, Cormack, and O'Brien 95). As Swan remarks, "it is not possible to provide simple 'recipes' to counteract them" [gender inequalities] (159).

Just as in society, the struggle for social justice through education requires multiple approaches. Appleman argues that "critical encounters with literary theory" will help "students to read the world around them"; these encounters "will help us name our theories and consider multiple perspectives as we find our place in the texts we read and the lives we lead" (147). In addition to reading the world in texts, Christensen calls for writing the world (62-65). Swann sees the monitoring of students' reading choices and types of writing as a way to reinforce readings of resistance (162). I believe that resistance is negotiated constantly because of the force of conformity, the desire to avoid punishment and social ostracism, the need to protect oneself emotionally by acquiescing or compromising, and many other reasons. One educational activity empowers a student, but that student may be oppressed in a situation in real life that parallel the situation encountered in that activity. Connections across disciplinary boundaries enlarge the students' frame of reference and help them see their experiences as shared with others. This is one of the principles of unity in social movements, such as the women's movement and feminist awareness. Sharing one's experiences in the confined environment of a classroom or the context of a story is not enough. The student needs to know where she or he is situated in the world as well. As Christensen reminds us, the written text (cartoons, literary stories), and I would add, the oral text, "legitimates what Chilean writer Ariel Dorfman (7) calls a 'social blueprint' about it means to be men, women, poor, people of color, gay, or straight. And that vision is political—whether it portrays the status quo or argues for a reorganization of society" (54).

¹ According to Foucault, there has emerged a series of practices against the body that aim at not only securing political allegiance or the products it produces but also control its elements, gestures, and behaviors. As the modern forms of coercion were developing, "the human body was entering a machinery of power that explores it, breaks it down and re-arranges it. A 'political anatomy', which was also a 'mechanics of power', was being born; it defined how one may have a hold over others' bodies, not only so that they may do what one wishes, but so that they may operate as one wishes, with the techniques, the speed and the efficiency that one determines. Thus, discipline produces subjected and practiced bodies, 'docile' bodies" (138).

² I am not advocating requiring children to bring specific items or materials for a school assignment or project. Families' cultural practices and material conditions differ, and such a requirement may result in undue burden on students and families. However, teachers should take advantage of items and materials children bring on their own and encourage personal connections for the purpose of teaching and learning.

³ "Nossos corpos estão sempre expostos a alguma espécie de leitura que os divide em têrmos de gênero. Por isso, sempre se materializam como corpos sexualizados."

4 These studies are known by other names, including queer linguistics. Some useful references are Campbell-Kibler, Kathryn, Robert J. Podesva, Sarah J. Roberts, and Andrew Wong's *Language and Sexuality: Contesting Meaning in Theory and Practice*. San Francisco: CSLI Publications, 2001; Leonard Ahsley's "Kinks and Queens: Linguistic and Cultural Aspects of the Terminology for Gays" in *Maledicta* 3 (1979): 215-56; John Champagne's "Seven Speculations on Queers and Class" in *Journal of Homosexuality* 26.1 (1993): 159-175; Judy Gahn's *Another Mother Tongue*. Boston: Beacon Press, 1994; Paula Treichler's "AIDS, Homophobia, and Biomedical Discourse: An Epidemic of Signification" in *AIS: Cultural Analysis, Cultural Activism*. Ed. Douglas Crimp, MIT Press, 1998. 31-37; and Joel Wells' "Sexual Language Usage in Different Interpersonal Contexts: A Comparison of Gender and Sexual Orientation" in *Archives of Sexual Behavior* 18.2 (1989) 127-44.

Works Cited

Allport, Gordon. "The Language of Prejudice." *Language Awareness*. Ed. Paul Eschholz, Alfred Rosa, and Virginia Clark. New York: St. Martin's Press, 1990. 247-56.

Appleman, Deborah. *Critical Encounters in High School English*. New York: Teachers College Press and NCTE, 2000.

Black, Maria and Rosalind Coward. "Linguistic, Sexual and Social Relations: A Review of Dale Spender's *Man Made Language*." *The Feminist Critique of Language*. Ed. Deborah Cameron. New York: Routledge, 1998. 100-18.

Bruffee, Kenneth. *Collaborative Learning: Higher Education, Interdependence and the Authority of Knowledge*. Baltimore: John Hopkins UP, 1993.

Cameron, Deborah. *The Feminist Critique of Language*. New York: Routledge, 1998.

Comber, Barbara and Helen Nixon. "Literacy Education as a Site for Social Justice: What Do Our Practices Do?" *Trends & Issues in Elementary Language Arts*, 2000. 117-47.

Comber, Barbara, Phil Cormack, and Jennifer O'Brien. "Schooling Disruptions: The Case of Critical Literacy." *The Fate of Progressive Language Policies and Practices.* Ed. Curt Dudley-Marling and Carole Edelsky. New York: NCTE, 2001. 83-104.

Comfort, Nathaniel C. "Two Genes, No Enzyme: a Second Look at Barbara McClintock and the 1951 Cold Spring Harbor Symposium." *Genetics* (1995) 140: 1161-66.

Costa, Jurandir Freire. *A Face e o Verso. Estudos sobre o homeorotismo II.* São Paulo: Escuta, 1995.

Christensen, Linda. "Critical Literacy: Teaching Reading, Writing, and Outrage." *Trends & Issues in Secondary English.* New York: NCTE, 2000. 53-66.

Dorfman, A. *The Empire's Old clothes: What the Lone Ranger, Babar, and Other Innocent Heroes Do to Our Minds.* New York: Pantheon, 1983.

Foucault, Michel. *Discipline and Punish: The Birth of Prison.* Trans. Alan Sheridan. New York: Vintage Books, 1979.

Fox Keller, Evelyn. *A Feeling for the Organism.* New York: WH Freeman, 1983.

Gee, James Paul. "Progressivism, Critique, and Socially Situated Minds." *The Fate of Progressive Language Policies and Practices*. Ed. Curt Dudley-Marling and Carole Edelsky. New York: NCTE, 2001. 31-58.

Martino, Wayne and Bronwyn Mellor. *Gendered Fictions*. New York: National Council of Teachers of English, 2000.

McKay, S.L., & Wong, S.-L.C. (1996). "Multiple Discourses, Multiple Identities: Investment and Agency in Second-Language Learning among Chinese Adolescent Immigrant Students." *Harvard Educational Review* 66.3 (1996): 577-608.

McClure, Lisa. "Language Activities that Promote Gender Fairness." *Gender Issues in the Teaching of English*. Ed. Nancy McCracken and Bruce C. Appleby. Portsmouth: Boyton/Cook, 1992. 39-50.

Moss, Gemma. *Unpopular/Fictions*. London: Virago, 1989.

Peirce, B.N. "Social Identity, Investment, and Language Learning." *TESOL Quarterly* 29.1 (1995): 9-31.

Pinker, Steven. *The Language Instinct. How the Mind Creates Language*. New York: Harper Collins, 1994.

Ramalho, Tania. "Teaching Foundations of Education from a Social Justice Perspective." Unpublished conference paper, 2001.

Rich, Adrienne. *Blood, Bread, and Poetry: Selected Prose, 1979-1985.* New York: W.W. Norton & Company, 1986.

Rosa, Rosana. "A terceira margem – corpo Negro." *Corpo e Cultura.* Ed. B. Lyra and W. Garcia. São Paulo: Xamã VM Editora and Gráfica, 2001. 39-46.

Santos, Ricardo. "O corpo queer." *Corpo e Cultura.* Ed. B. Lyra and W. Garcia. São Paulo: Xamã VM Editora and Gráfica, 2001. 103-08.

Swann, Joan. *Girls, Boys, & Language.* Cambridge: Blackwell, 1995.

Thompson, John B. "Editor's Introduction." By Pierre Bourdieu. *Language and Symbolic Power.* Cambridge, MA: Harvard University Press, 1991. 1-31.

Van Den Bergh, Nan. "Re-naming: Vehicle for Empowerment." *Women and Language in Transition.* Ed. Joyce Penfield. Albany: State University of New York Press, 1987.

West, Cornell. *Race Matters.* Boston: Beacon Press, 1993. Willinsky, John. "What is Progressive about Progressive Education?" *The Fate of Progressive Language Policies and Practices.* New York: NCTE, 2001. 59-79.

Young, Iris M. *Justice and the Politics of Difference.* Princeton: Princeton University Press, 1990.

In some areas of Chile undergoing agrarian reform the peasants participating in the literacy programs wrote words with their tools on the dirt road where they were working. "These men are sowers of the word," said a sociologist. Indeed, they were not only sowing words, but discussing ideas, and coming to understand their role in the world better and better.

Paolo Freire

Pedagogy of the Oppressed

Writers from the War Zone: Poets and the Literature of the Northern Ireland Troubles

Maureen Murphy

History has been a preoccupation of Irish poets since the Ulster hero Fergus mac Roig appeared to the poets to relate the Irish epic, the *Táin Bó Cuailnge*. The past was the poets' trust; their preservation, their duty. Contemporary Irish poets inherited this tradition and have brought their individual perspectives to their interpretation of the present troubles in Northern Ireland that are now in their thirty-fourth year. Some poets have written about the conflict in the fabric of their own lives; some try to place the events into a wider context of Irish history; others have used the Northern Irish experience to confront, explore and explain ideas about identity and community. The poems offer teachers and students ways to examine literature about a topic written from multiple perspectives that use poetic elements to create metaphors for understanding the nature of a particular conflict at the turn of the twenty-first century.

There are three dimensions to the conflict in Northern Ireland. One concerns civil rights and social justice. The second is political. Unionists wish to remain in the United Kingdom; Nationalists opt for a thirty-two county Republic of Ireland. The third embraces both; it is the matter of identity and community. Irish poets have responded most often to the matters of civil rights and community.

Inspired by the American civil rights movement, the Northern Ireland Civil Rights movement was founded in 1967 to address the systematic, sectarian discrimination in employment and the allocation of rented accommodation in chronically scarce public housing. In his poem "A New Siege," part of John Montague's *A Rough Field 1961-1971*, a historical meditation on the Ulster past that contrasts the Siege of Derry in 1689, where Catholics held Protestants within the walls of the city, with the battle of Bogside in August 1969. This time the Catholics were under siege, confined within their Bogside neighborhood by Protestants after a clash over a yearly parade that celebrated the seventeenth century Protestant victory in Derry. Montague identifies the 1969 Battle of Bogside not as a unique Irish moment but as a moment in the world of the 1960s when the American civil rights movement fired another "shot heard round the world." He describes the "lines of protest" that stretched from Berkeley to Belfast, as part of the "seismic waves/zigzagging through a faulty world."

Like their American counterparts, civil rights activists were attacked by police during nonviolent demonstrations. Derry poet Seamus Deane spent his teenage years on the bitter streets of the Bogside. His poem "Derry" (*Gradual Wars* 1972) begins with a line that describes the violence that erupts from injustice:
>The unemployment in our bones
>Erupting on our hands in stones (29, ll. 1-2).

Confrontations between civil rights activists escalated. The government tried to contain the violence by banning demonstrations and marches; however, British paratroopers fired on civilian protestors in Derry on January 30, 1972, killing thirteen, many of whom were boys of seventeen. Deane described the stunned young of the community after "Bloody Sunday" in "After Derry, 30 January 1972," Section 6 of his "Fourteen Elegies,":

There are new children
In the gaunt houses.
Their eyes are fused.
Youth has gone out
Like a light (Deane 16, ll. 12-17)

Republic of Ireland poet Thomas Kinsella responded to Bloody Sunday with *Butcher's Dozen*, a pamphlet poem published a week after the Widgery Tribunal issued its report exonerating the military. The tone of the poem's octosyllabic couplets shares Swift's *sava indignatio*:

Simple lessons cut most deep.
This lesson in our hearts we keep:
Persuasion, protest. arguments,
The milder forms of violence,
Earns nothing but polite neglect.
England, the way to your respect
Is via murderous force, it seems;
You push us to your own extremes (Kinsella 16, ll . 32-39).

Seamus Heaney has looked at the troubles in Northern Ireland through overlapping lenses of Irish history, Irish identity and Irish community. While Heaney marched in early civil rights demonstrations organized by his old school friend, the constitutional nationalist John Hume, he stayed away from the political rhetoric of poems like *Butcher's Dozen*. His decision was not without risk, a risk he describes in his poem "Exposure" where the poet wonders whether his relocation from Northern Ireland to rural Wicklow where he has "Escaped from the massacre," and his preoccupation with the "meagre heat" of his poetry has caused him to miss "The once-in-a-lifetime portent." But he does not miss the experience of his generation; he finds wider ways to frame that experience.[1]

The poems in Heaney's 1975 collection *North* mine the metaphors in the architectural and archaeological remains of Ireland and northern Europe for ways to make meaning and to suggest new solutions to the violence in Northern Ireland. In "Funeral Rites" Heaney describes the traditional customs associated with death in the Irish countyside, and he calls for new rituals for the victims of "neighborly murders." Heaney proposes that the dead of sectarian violence be returned to the megalithic tombs of the Boyne Valley, a place that predates the coming of "planted" English and Scottish colonists to Northern Ireland. The image of the Scandinavian hero whose death breaks the cycle of revenge suggests an allusion to the Oresteia with its evolution from vendetta and murder to a system of public justice.

Heaney understands the complicated nature of the relationship within and between the communities and that violation of their mores results in terrifying penalties. In "Punishment," Heaney conflates the image of the Windeby Girl, a young adultress found preserved perfectly in a northern European bog, with young nationalist woman tarred and feathered and chained to a fence for fraternizing with a British soldier. Ancient ritual meets contemporary ritual. The poet charges himself with the sin of silence ("I who have stood dumb"); he both condemns the punishment and understands its "exact" and "tribal" nature.[2]

Heaney's understanding of his people is rooted in his nationalist reading of history. In an interview with Elgy Gillespie in *The Irish Times* (19 May 1972), Heaney spoke of the shaping force of history on his work:

I have been writing poems out of history. It is the hump we live off. I have my taproot in personal and racial memory. The Famine, the '98 rebellion—things like that—have surfaced in my imagination and they are living language here.

History as language/language as history has special implications for Ireland. The Irish language lost by conquest and then by domination (as English threatens many minority languages today), nonetheless continues to be an essential part of Irish identity.[3] While James Joyce's Stephen Daedalus refuses to study Irish with his Gaelic Leaguer friends, he recognizes that as an Irishman, English is not really his first language, and it unsettles him. As he talks about a *tundish* with the Dean of Studies in the fire-lighting scene in *A Portrait of the Artist as a Young Man*. Stephen broods:

> His language, so familiar and so foreign will always be for me an acquired speech. I have not made or accepted its words. My voice holds them at bay. My soul frets in the shadow of his language.

Heaney revisits the issues of language and culture in "Traditions." He refers to the coming of the Normans to Ireland in 1172, the beginning of colonization that was politically fixed by the Act of Union (between Great Britain and Ireland) in 1800. One consequence of English colonialism was the shift from the Irish language to English.

Part II of the poem charts the survivals of archaic English vocabulary and pronunciation in Ireland and the influence of the Irish language on spoken English. For example, in the Irish language, an *s* next to an *i* or an *e* is pronounced *sh*. (Think of the boy's name Sean which is pronounced *Shawn*.)

In Part III, Heaney answers MacMorris's question "What ish my nation?" with a quote from Joyce, not the anxious narcissistic Stephen Daedalus but the decent, compassionate Leopold Bloom, the hero of *Ulysses*. Bloom is baited by the chauvinistic Citizen, a catholic, Irish-speaking nationalist who can not accept that Bloom, a Dublin-born Jew, is an Irishman. Bullying Bloom, the Citizen demands, "What is your nation if I may ask?" For Heaney, Bloom answers "sensibly." "Ireland. I was born here. Ireland."

Heaney's use of Bloom's response, his expression of inclusiveness, is not merely a literary allusion. Heaney speaks to the need for his native Northern Ireland to move beyond the divisive issues of identity and culture to create a community based on a wider definition of what it means to be Irish.[4]

While Heaney has explored Catholic nationalist identity and argued for a more inclusive Irishness, Louis MacNeice, W.R. Rodgers and John Hewitt have considered the identity of the Protestant Northern community. The title of Rodger's "Home Thoughts from Abroad" is an ironic borrowing from Robert Browning's romantic poem of spring in England. Rodgers observes, from England, the reports of Northern Ireland exploding with the thunder of old invective. He compares the hard-line Unionist minister Ian Paisley "eyeless in Gaza" to John Milton's *Samson Agonistes*.

MacNeice and Rodgers were not preoccupied with defining the Northern Irish protestant. John Hewitt, on the other hand, wrote about the protestant planters of the Glens of Antrim, finding in them an authentic Ulster voice.

Influenced by Robert Frost's poem "The Gift Outright," with its opening lines that described the dilemma of colonial people living on the land but not of the land, Hewitt's poem "Once Alien Here" begins with a similar experience:
> Once alien here my fathers built their house,
> Claimed, drained, and gave the land the shapes of use (Hewitt 22, ll. 1-2).

His poem "O Country People" suggests that any accommodation made with land does not extend to the native Irish:
> I would be neighborly, would come to terms
> with your existence, but you are so far;
> there is a bog between us, a high wall (Hewitt 69, ll. 5-7).

The poets of community: wider Irish identity and neighborliness contributed to the commitment to peace expressed by the people of Northern Ireland when they voted to approve the Good Friday Agreement in 1998. Michael Longley set the tone for the post-Good Friday North with his sonnet "Ceasefire" which was published in *The Irish Times* the next day. The poem is not about the ceasefire in Northern Ireland but the end of the Trojan War. In describing a meeting of reconciliation between old enemies: Achilles weeping with Priam, returns Hector's corpse properly cleaned and dressed and, Priam responds with his own gesture of reconciliation:
> I get down on my knees and do what must be done
> And kiss Achilles' hand, the killer of my son (Longley 18, ll. 13-14).

A lasting peace in Northern Ireland continues to be elusive; however, poets continue to offer metaphors of reconciliation within the community and with history.

Among the other voices who have written about Northern Ireland are young people who have described what it has meant to grow up in the terror of a divided community where violence is the ordinary. Aine da Silva's "Self-Preservation" outlines the strategies of survival Northern teenagers develop:

> We know where we are not supposed to walk.
> Our Christian names and surnames betray us across enemy lines.
>
> But we have learned the hard way
> we know the time and place for lies.
>
> We are the experts of self-preservation.
> Children of the cold war.
> Children of the Troubles.
> Our bombs are close but they are not quite nuclear although they steal our families from us (Holliday 99. ll. 9-18).

Other young poets describe the way that the Troubles divided communities shattering friendships. Fourteen year-old Pasqualina Johnston describes a lost friendship in "The Other Side":

> Now when we meet
> We never speak
> For fear of the boys in the street

Because she's of the "other side" (Holliday 160, ll. 8-11).

Others like Larragh Cullen, age eleven, yearn for peace that has not come in her life time:

> I live in Dungannon,
> I've never known peace,
> I'm tired of choppers,
> Soldiers and police.
>
> I'm tired of the sirens
> The town is a cage,
> I wish there was peace,
> I'm eleven years of age (Holliday 167. ll. 5-12).

These examples are the work of children caught in the crossfire, children in contemporary war zones. Literature of other adolescents in similar circumstances like Zlata Filiparvic's diary, shares the sorrow of broken communities. All share a common hope for peace; all have a profound sense of place and the dislocation brought by war; all yearn for normalcy. Because these adolescents are not cut off from the world, they express concern for the suffering of others, for the environment and for the future of their generation.

The literature of conflict in Northern Ireland that describes a generation of civil unrest offers a great deal of material for adolescent and young adult readers. The following bibliography of the adolescent in the Northern Ireland conflict literature is designed for the high school classroom and covers a range of topics and genre as well as background literature and resources. The common feature is the focus on the way that conflict affects the adolescent protagonist or speaker.

[1] Heaney revisited "Exposure" in his 1995 Nobel Prize speech, "Crediting Poetry." "What I was longing for was not quite stability but an active escape from the quicksand of relativism, a way of crediting poetry without anxiety or apology." (Heaney *Crediting* 14).

[2] Jennifer Johnston's novel, *Shadows on Our Skin* (1977), deals with such a local and tribal punishment.

[3] The most significant historical statements about the importance of the Irish language to national identity is Thomas Davis's essay "Our National Language" (1843) and Douglas Hyde's "The Necessity for De-Anglicizing Ireland" (1892). Brian Friel's play, *Translations* (1981), which is set in rural Donegal in 1833, during the Ordnance Survey project which replaced traditional Irish place names with their English approximations, considers the far-reaching influence on culture and national identity. John Montague's poem, "A Grafted Tongue," describes the custom of punishing children for speaking Irish and uses the practice as a metaphor for the humiliation he suffered as a stuttering boy.

[4] Writing about these passages, students have discussed how language "made one character feel disconnected," "created a personal dilemma about what language one

should speak and how a person feels about making such a decision," "helped make it possible to accept one's heritage," "asked questions about whether one has to speak a particular language to be considered a member of a society," and "showed that some people were not proud of their native language."

Selected Readings

Anthology:
Holliday, Laurel. *Children of "The Troubles."* New York: Pocket Books, 1997.
Holliday has collected stories, diaries, autobiographical writings and poems about growing up in Northern Ireland during the last thirty years.

Fiction:
Johnston, Jennifer. *Shadows on our Skin.* London: Hamish Hamilton, 1977.
Fontanta paperback, 1988. Joe Logan lives in Derry, a city troubled by sectarian violence. He befriends Kathleen Doherty, a lonely schoolteacher who is in love with a young soldier in the British Army. Joe's brother, on the run with the IRA, returns to Derry, meets Kathleen and is attracted to her. An impulsive, angry word from Joe destroys Joe's innocence and sends Kathleen from Derry. Teach with Seamus Heaney's poem "Punishment" (*Selected Poems*) 1980, pp. 192-93 and the Louis Malle film *Au Revoir les Enfants* (1987).

MacLaverty, Bernard. *Cal*. New York: George Braziller, 1983.
Cal McClusky, an unemployed Belfast youth, drifts into the IRA. First there are robberies; then, Cal drives the get-away car in a the murder an Robert Morton, a Royal Irish Constabulary reservist. Cal hears the dying man scream "Marcella;" later, when he is attracted to a young woman in his local library, he is horrified to hear her called Marcella. Attracted to her, Cal must come to terms with his part in Marton's death. Teach with selected portions of "Cal" (director: Pat O'Connor) and with Bernard Malamud's *The Assistant*.

Madden, Deirdre. *Hidden Symptoms*. Boston: Atlantic Monthly, 1986.
Belfast college student Theresa tries to make sense of her life after her twin brother Francis is brutally murdered by terrorists. She faces a crisis of faith in a world of random and senseless violence.

Poetry:
Bardwell, Leland. *Borderlines 2. Poems by Young People in the Border Area*. Beech Hill, Monaghan: County Monaghan Vocational Education Committee, 1994.
A collection of eighty poems by adolescents in the counties that border Northern Ireland and the Republic of Ireland that address the issues of community, peace, violence, cultural identity and the environment.

Deane, Seamus. *Gradual Wars*. Shannon: Irish University Press, 1972.

Heaney, Seamus. *Opened Ground. Poems 1966-1996*. London: Faber and Faber, 1998.

Hewitt, John. *Collected Poems 1932-67*. London: Macgibbon and Kee, 1969.

Kinsella, Thomas. *Fifteen Dead*. New York: Oxford University Press, 1979.

Longley, Michael. *Selected Poems*. Winston-Salem: Wake Forest University Press, 1999.

Autobiography and Biography:
Adams, Gerry. *Falls Memories*. Niwot, CO: Roberts Rinehart Publisher, 1994.
Adams is President of *Sinn Fein*, the Irish Republican political party. He is widely believed to have been a member of the outlawed Irish Republican Army. His autobiography describes growing up in the Catholic, nationalist Falls Road section of Belfast.

Devlin, Bernadette. *The Price of My Soul*. New York: Knopf, 1969.
Devlin's account of her childhood and youth in Northern Ireland and the forces that brought her into the civil rights movement and ultimately to her election to Parliament.

White,Barry. *John Hume. Statesman of the Troubles.* Belfast: The Blackstaff Press, 1984. John Hume has lead the party of moderate, constitutional nationalism from the streets of Derry, to Westminster and to Europe. The architect of the civil rights movement in Derry and the peace process that resulted in the Good Friday Agreement, Hume shared the Nobel Peace Prize in 1998 with Unionist leader David Trimble.

Background Reading:
Cairns, Edward. *Caught in the Crossfire. Children and the Northern Ireland Conflict.* Syracuse: Syracuse University Press.

Carolyn. *Voices of Northern Ireland. Growing Up in a Troubled Land.* San Diego: Gullilver Books, 1973.

Rosenblatt, Roger. *Children of War.* London: New English Library, 1973.

Van Voris, W.H. *Violence in Ulster. An Oral Documentary.* Amherst: University of Massachusetts Press, 1975.

Film:
"Hush-a-Bye Baby." Margo Harkins. 1989. 80 minutes. Goretti, a fifteen year old girl, living in troubled Derry in 1984 discovers she is pregnant. Her boyfriend has been interred by the British Army.

"The End of the World Man." Bill Miskelly. 1985. 82 minutes.
Two ten year old girls, one Catholic and one Protestant, work together to save a Belfast park.

Meet the Authors

Regina Derrico, English Department chairperson at Williamsville East High School in New York State, has extensive experiences both publishing and presenting issues related to English education. She has delivered conference presentations for NCTE, the National Reading Conference, the New York State Reading Association, and the New York State English Council. Regina also teaches in the Graduate School of Education at the University at Buffalo--SUNY in the Division of Learning and Instruction.

In addition to teaching, Regina is active in professional organizations. She is a member of the Secondary Section Steering Committee of NCTE, in addition to serving as Membership Chairperson for the New York State English Council.

Rob Linné teaches at Adelphi University campuses in Manhattan and Long Island. He received a Ph.D. from the University of Texas at Austin. His areas of specialization include young adult literature and narrative research. Questions or comments can be sent to linne@adelphi.edu.

Laurie Iodice received her B.A. in English from City University of New York and her M.S. in English Education from Syracuse University. She has just completed her twenty-fifth year in the classroom and has taught in a wide range of educational settings, both on the secondary level and on the post-secondary level, at Syracuse University. During her tenure there, she also served as a professional development coordinator and as consultant for Syracuse

University's Project Advance. Her most recent appointment is at Fayetteville-Manlius High School where she teaches Syracuse University Project Advance English and Interdisciplinary Honors English.

Originally from New York City, Laurie and her husband settled in Syracuse shortly after completing their undergraduate studies and have been local residents ever since.

Melissa Hasbrook is a Ph.D. candidate in Critical Studies in the Teaching of English at Michigan State University. Focusing on activist research, her work examines individuals negotiating educational institutions, especially by working-class older students. Her current projects include collaborative inquiry and reflection in Freirean pedagogy. While teaching humanities, writing, and teacher education at MSU, she also has worked at Tutoring Services of Lansing Community College. Melissa participates in labor advocacy efforts with the Conference on College Composition and Communication and conference planning for the Michigan Developmental Education Consortium.

Alice Trupe teaches young adult literature and other courses required for preservice teachers at Bridgewater College of Virginia, where she also directs the Writing Center and first-year composition. Her research interests include Asian-American literature and the effective integration of computers into classroom instruction.

Ines Senna Shaw, a Brazilian-American with a Ph.D. in linguistics, teaches ESL, composition, literature, linguistics, women's studies, and Latin American studies at SUNY-affiliated Nassau Community College. Her main research interest is gender and language from an integrated sociolinguistic, historical, and feminist perspective.

Maureen Murphy is Professor of Curriculum and Teaching at Hofstra University. A specialist in Irish literature, she is the Director of the *Great Irish Famine Project* for the New York State Education Department. She has written and lectured widely about Irish literature, history, folklore, comparative literature and mythology. Maureen is also Vice-President--College of the New York State English Council.

John Harmon is the Humanities Curriculum Coordinator for the Skaneateles Central School District. His publications include articles in *English Studies* and *English Journal,* as well as a former issues of *The Monograph.* He is also the current President of the New York State English Council.